P9-CDG-356

BISON
BOOKS

GUERRILLA WARFARE

CHE GUEVARA

Introduction to the Bison Books Edition
by Marc Becker

UNIVERSITY OF NEBRASKA PRESS • LINCOLN

Manufactured in the United States of America

♾ The paper in this book meets the minimum requirements of American National Standard for Information Sciences—Permanence of Paper for Printed Library Materials, ANSI Z39.48-1984.

First Bison Books printing: 1998

Library of Congress Cataloging-in-Publication Data
Guevara, Ernesto, 1928–1967.
[Guerra de guerrillas. English]
Guerrilla warfare / Che Guevara; introduction to the Bison Books edition by Marc Becker.
p. cm.
Originally published: New York: Monthly Review Press, 1961.
Includes bibliographical references.
ISBN 0-8032-7075-5 (pbk.: alk. paper)
1. Guerrilla warfare—Latin America—Case studies. 2. Guerrilla warfare. I. Title.
U240.G8313 1998
355.02′18′098—dc21
98-19944 CIP

INTRODUCTION

Marc Becker

Thirty years after his death, university students throughout Latin America still wear T-shirts emblazoned with Che Guevara's image. Workers carry placards and banners featuring him as they march through the streets demanding higher wages and better working conditions. Zapatista guerrillas in southern Mexico paint murals depicting Che together with Emiliano Zapata and Indian heros. In Cuba, vendors sell Che watches to tourists. Not only has he captured the popular imagination, but recently several authors have written lengthy biographies detailing the revolutionary's life.[1] In the face of a political milieu that considers socialism to be a discredited ideology, what explains this continued international fascination with a guerrilla leader and romantic revolutionary who died in a failed attempt to spark a hemispheric Marxist insurrection?

Che's life represents a selfless dedication to the concerns of the underclass, a struggle to encourage people to place the needs of the broader society above their own narrow personal wishes and desires, and a willingness to make extensive personal sacrifices to achieve a more just and equable social order. Che made the ultimate sacrifice for his beliefs. With his death in October of 1967 at the hands of the military in Bolivia he became a martyr and a prophet for leftist causes and beliefs.

Che, however, is more a symbolic representation of these struggles than an intellectual or philosophical leader.[2] In fact, since the 1960s specific aspects of his thought (particularly his *foco* theory of guerrilla warfare) have become discredited. Over the last ten or fifteen years, new issues that Che never seriously considered, such as ethnic consciousness, have become critically important to popular movements for social justice. In the aftermath of seemingly endless and deadly guerrilla battles in the 1980s in Central America, Peru, and Colombia, many leftist political activists are now content to limit their struggles for social justice to the political arena rather than resorting to armed uprisings. In fact, many militants would now consider guerrilla warfare to be a failure that represents the breakdown of civil society. They strive to keep these fundamentally political issues in the arena in which they properly belong.

Che's *Guerrilla Warfare*, thus, is now seen in a different light than when it was originally written in 1960. It has become a historical document rather than a manual or blueprint for the overthrow of imperialism and capitalism. Nevertheless, it represents a significant stage in the development of leftist revolutionary thought in Latin America. In order to understand more accurately the revolutionary fervor of the 1960s, insurrectionary movements during the 1980s, and the current situation in Latin America, it is important to read, understand, and analyze this key historic document. This includes considering the life and personal history of its author and examining key points, contributions, and shortcomings of the document in light of intellectual trends within current popular movements in Latin America.

CHE GUEVARA: HIS LIFE AND TIMES

Che Guevara was born Ernesto Guevara de la Serna on June 14, 1928, to an aristocratic family in Rosario, Argentina. Years later, Cuban revolutionaries in Mexico gave him the nickname "Che," a word from the Guaraní Indians that is commonly used in Argentina and can be roughly translated as "hey you." In 1959, after the triumph of the Cuban Revolution, he became a Cuban citizen and legally adopted Che as part of his name. Che's family held leftist ideas, including opposition to the institutional power of the church and support for the Republicans in the Spanish Civil War. Che's mother, Celia de la Serna, had a particularly important influence on the formation of his social conscience. In 1948 he entered the University of Buenos Aires to study medicine. Although Che eventually finished medical school, he was never seriously committed to the profession. Almost a decade later, after landing in Cuba with Fidel Castro to launch an insurrectionary war against the Fulgencio Batista dictatorship, when forced to choose he decided to carry bullets rather than a first-aid kit.

In his early twenties, Che made two motorcycle trips during

which he directly observed the lives of workers and peasants for the first time. In 1950 he took a four-thousand-mile moped trip alone through northern Argentina. During 1951 and 1952 Che journeyed through South America on a 500cc Norton motorcycle nicknamed "La Poderosa" (The Powerful One) with Alberto Granado, a radical doctor and leprologist.[3] These trips introduced him to the political and economic realities of Latin America and the poverty and exploitation under which the majority of the Latin American people lived. It was a consciousness-raising experience that ultimately changed the direction his life would take.

In 1953 Che began a third trip through Latin America. In Bolivia he observed the mobilization of workers and the implementation of agrarian reform following the popular 1952 revolution. He then continued on to Guatemala, where he lived until a United States–backed coup overthrew the revolutionary government of Jacobo Arbenz in 1954. He gleaned important lessons from this experience, which would strongly influence his later ideology. He believed that it was necessary to destroy completely the political and military forces of the old system, something Arbenz had not done. Under Che's leadership, the Cuban revolutionaries eradicated all vestiges of Batistas's government and successfully maintained their hold on power. In contrast, the Sandinista guerrillas who triumphed in Nicaragua in 1979 did not do this and subsequently faced a drawn-out war against counterrevolutionary forces that eventually contributed to their fall from power. If Arbenz had had more faith in the Indians, peasants, and workers, Che contended, and had been willing to organize them into armed militias, the revolutionary government would have maintained power. The role of the United States in the coup in 1954 also turned Che into a dedicated fighter against United States imperialism in Latin America.

After the overthrow of Arbenz's revolutionary government in Guatemala, Che escaped to Mexico, where he met Fidel Castro, who was planning an invasion of his native Cuba. In Mexico Che began to study Marxism and became an ideological communist. Hilda Gadea, a political exile from Peru whom Che married, had a particularly strong influence on the development of his ideology. She introduced Che to many new political and intellectual ideas, including those of José Carlos Mariátegui, the founder of Latin American Marxist thought. These ideological influences had a dramatic impact on his later development as a Marxist thinker.[4]

Che joined Fidel and his small guerrilla army in 1956 when they traveled to Cuba's eastern region to begin a guerrilla war against the Batista regime. Che, chosen because of his medical skills, was the only non-Cuban included in this group. For two years Che fought alongside Fidel in the Sierra Maestra mountains of Cuba, eventually rising to the rank of Rebel Army commander. During this time he solidified the revolutionary ideologies and military strategies that would later form the basis for *Guerrilla Warfare*.

After the triumph of the Cuban Revolution on January 1, 1959, Che assumed a series of positions in the new government. He was first named to head the national bank, a job for which he had no training or expertise. In 1961 he assumed the post of minister of industry. He led a Cuban delegation to the Inter-American Economic and Social Council sponsored by the Organization of American States in Uruguay, where he strongly denounced the motives of John F. Kennedy's Alliance for Progress program.[5] The Alliance for Progress was a ten-year development program that sought, through mild social and economic reforms, to prevent in other Latin American countries radical social revolutions such as that in Cuba. In fact, Che's *Guerrilla Warfare* probably led Kennedy to his conclusion that those who make peaceful change impossible make violent revolution inevitable.

Increasingly, Che traveled internationally as an ambassador for Cuba. He left Cuba in 1965 to spread the revolutionary struggle. He first surfaced in Africa fighting in the Congo and then returned to Latin America with the intent of sparking a hemisphere-wide guerrilla uprising. Che became increasingly vocal in denouncing United States imperialism. He believed that people throughout Latin America were ready for a revolutionary uprising. In his last public statement, a message to the Organization of Solidarity with the Peoples of Asia, Africa, and Latin America (OSPAAAL, also known as the Tricontinental), he spoke of creating "two, three, or many Vietnams," which would strike a deadly blow against imperialism. Much like Simón Bolívar and José Martí before him, Che was a true internationalist who believed that the destiny of Latin America was singular and unified. National borders simply served to divide people in their struggle to achieve a more just social order.

Che chose Bolivia as the place to launch this pan-American war, more because of its strategic geographic location than out of concern for local conditions. Despite the presence of a radical Marxist urban labor movement possibly sympathetic to his political ideologies, he chose to position his guerrilla army in Bolivia's isolated eastern jungle, which was more appropriate to his military strategy. Emphasizing geography over subjective political ideologies turned out to be a costly mistake. Che alienated the Bolivian Communist Party based in La Paz, depriving him of a critically important base of support for his efforts. Moreover, the Guaraní Indians living in the sparsely populated eastern jungle had received land in a government-sponsored agrarian reform program and felt little animosity toward the Bolivian army (members of which were often recruited from their own ranks). The local population had few reasons to defend a foreign guerrilla army that was culturally different, did not speak their language, and did not reflect local concerns. Ironically, in a short essay from 1963 entitled "Guerrilla Warfare: A Method," Che emphasized the importance of popular support to a guerrilla struggle. Without this backing, a disaster was inevitable.

For several months, Che engaged in skirmishes with the Bolivian military but was always on the defensive. On October 8, 1967, the army captured Che and his few remaining guerrilla fighters near the small village of La Higuera. The next day they executed him and publicly displayed his body. In death he looked like a sacrificed Christ, which helped create an image of Che as a martyr and prophet. A popular cult grew around "Saint Ernesto of La Higuera," and locals placed his portrait in their houses alongside Catholic images. The army buried his body in a mass grave, where it remained until it was repatriated to Cuba in 1997 with a hero's welcome. Since his death, Che's supporters have celebrated October 8 as the Day of the Heroic Guerrilla.[6] Like Eva Perón, Che became a more potent symbol in death than he had ever been in life.

Che's death ushered in a year of violent repression of political opposition movements around the world. In April and June of 1968 assassins killed civil rights leader Martin Luther King

Jr. and presidential candidate Robert Kennedy in the United States. During May student and worker protests paralyzed Paris, France. In August Chicago police attacked Vietnam War protestors at the Democratic National Convention. The Mexican army shot an estimated three hundred protestors in October at the Plaza of Three Cultures in Mexico City. Che's death did not mean the end of revolutionary actions, and it only helped to polarize further an already tense global political situation.

GUERRILLA WARFARE

Guerrilla Warfare is an extended essay that runs well over one hundred pages. Che published it in May of 1960, about a year after the triumph of the Cuban Revolution. It is divided into three chapters that outline the general principles of guerrilla warfare, describe the nature of a guerrilla group, and explain the strategies of a guerrilla army. A manual setting forth his ideas on conducting a guerrilla war to overthrow a dictatorship and implement a new and more just social order, it is part theory, part practical information (though over time much of this information has become outdated), and part a political tract designed to press the Left into action. He speaks directly from his experience helping Fidel and Raul Castro organize their guerrilla army in Cuba. At times he considers this history to be normative, yet at other points he indicates that Cuba's experience is only an outline; other guerrilla forces would have to discover paths suitable to their own situations. Generally, though, Che analyzed the Cuban Revolution in order to extract general laws and develop a theory of guerrilla warfare.

Many historians see the Cuban Revolution as a watershed event in twentieth-century Latin American history, and Che lays out what he believes is the historical significance of their guerrilla victory. First, it demonstrated that people can organize themselves into a small guerrilla army and overthrow a large, powerful, established regime. Second, popular movements do not have to wait for the proper economic conditions before organizing a revolutionary war; the insurrectionary guerrilla force can create them. Third, Latin American revolutionary struggles should, according to Che, be based in a rural, peasant population. These three concepts underlie this entire work, and it is worth examining them in more detail.

In order to understand the theoretical and political implications of Che's major points, it is important to understand the international context of the Cuban Revolution. Although the United States consistently blamed leftist uprisings in Latin America on the Soviet Union's penetration of "its" hemisphere, the Cuban Revolution did not begin as a communist movement. In fact, the Cuban Communist Party denounced the guerrillas as "adventuresome." Since the 1930s, communist parties in Latin America generally had pursued a gradualist "Popular Front" strategy in which they sought slowly to build a base of support within established political structures. They fostered peaceful relations with existing moderate governments, even to the point of accepting positions in those governments. Che, on the other hand, believed that a vanguardist group with strong leadership could grab power. He became highly critical of bureaucratic Soviet communism, which had lost its revolutionary fervor. Che believed in a revolutionary movement that responded to local conditions, not the geopolitical concerns of a distant empire.

Related to this strategic difference with the communists are two important ideological distinctions. Karl Marx believed that history moved through a series of stages, from a feudalistic stage through capitalism to the final perfect stage of communism. Although in the 1917 Russian Revolution Vladimir Lenin had demonstrated that feudalistic societies could move immediately to the communist stage, orthodox Marxists in Latin America still believed that an industrialized capitalist economy was essential before workers would gain the necessary class consciousness to break loose from their chains and overthrow an oppressive system. Che, however, following in the footsteps of earlier Latin American Marxist thinkers such as José Carlos Mariátegui, belived that subjective conditions, including the role of human consciousness, were more important for creating a revolutionary situation than the objective economic situation.[7] To spur the revolution a dedicated cadre must engage in the political education of the masses rather than wait for a highly developed capitalist economy to collapse due to its internal contradictions. "The duty of every revolutionary is to make the revolution," Fidel Castro later stated. "It is known that the revolution will triumph in America and throughout the world, but it is not for revolutionaries to sit in the doorways of their houses waiting for the corpse of imperialism to pass by."[8]

Mariátegui, Che, and other Latin American Marxists also broke with orthodox thought over the role of the peasantry in a revolutionary movement. In the *Communist Manifesto*, Marx wrote that the peasantry was "not revolutionary, but conservative." He proceeded to note that "nay more, they are reactionary, for they try to roll back the wheel of history."[9] Latin America, however, largely lacked an urban, industrialized working class, which orthodox Marxists believed would lead a socialist revolution. Instead, in the 1950s landless agricultural workers comprised much of Latin America's population. Although Marx thought that peasants were inactive, passive like a "sack of potatoes," Che believed they could head a revolutionary movement.[10] Che believed that the experience of the Cuban Revolution demonstrated that peasants understood the nature of their exploitation and were able to achieve the class consciousness necessary to engage in revolutionary action. As Eric Wolf demonstrated in *Peasant Wars of the Twentieth Century*, successful revolutionary movements in Mexico, Russia, China, Vietnam, and Algeria as well as in Cuba have been rural based.[11]

The most controversial aspect of Che's thought, the one that many people believe led to his eventual defeat and execution in Bolivia, was his belief that a guerrilla force could create the objective conditions necessary for a guerrilla war. Previous revolutionary theorists had argued that certain political and economic conditions were necessary for a successful struggle. In what became known as his *foco* theory of guerrilla warfare, Che argued that a small guerrilla army operating in the countryside could spark a revolution that would then spread to the cities. Only a handful of guerrillas in each country was necessary to begin a process that would transform Latin America. This led him in *Guerrilla Warfare* to emphasize the importance of a proper geographic setting for an armed struggle. A jungle environment that provided good cover for the guerrillas was more important than the ideological preparation of a large civilian base of support.

Che's *foco* theory subsequently was discredited in Latin America; those who attempted to implement it failed miserably.

In Peru in 1965, Héctor Béjar's insurrectionary *foco* met defeat, and two years later Che himself was killed while attempting to follow this strategy in Bolivia.[12] Many people have criticized Che for overemphasizing the role of armed struggle in a revolutionary movement and have pointed out that, although a relatively small guerrilla force overthrew Batista in Cuba, this came only after years of leftist political agitations and rising worker expectations.[13] Because of his role in guerrilla battles in the mountains, he either was not aware of or discounted a coalition of urban student and worker movements that served to undermine the Batista regime. A lengthy debate has also ensued suggesting that Che misidentified the rural masses of Cuba as a peasant population. They worked primarily as wage laborers on large plantations and therefore comprised a rural proletariat that had developed a class consciousness unlike that which a more traditional peasantry could be expected to develop.[14]

Many of the ideas in *Guerrilla Warfare* were not new; what Che did contribute to revolutionary theory was a creative adaptation of existing notions to the Latin American context. He did not realize, however, how unique the Cuban situation was and his defeat in Bolivia was a result of a failure to reinterpret what he had learned for a new and different situation. Subsequent guerrilla armies learned from the fiasco in Bolivia to reinterpret Che's theories for their own local reality and never to apply mechanically what had worked in one situation to another.

ETHNICITY AND NEW GUERRILLA STRUGGLES IN LATIN AMERICA

Che grew up in an urban milieu in Argentina in which he was not constantly and directly exposed to the daily battles that Latin America's large rural Indigenous and peasant population faced. He encountered this rural reality as an adult traveling through Latin America and in the Sierra Maestra of Cuba. He interpreted it through an outsider's *indigenista* perspective that betrayed sympathy for Indian and peasant causes, but he was not able to internalize their struggles or analyze the world from an Indigenous person's point of view. On his motorcycle trip through South America, Che visited the Inca ruins at Machu Picchu in the Peruvian highlands. He was impressed with the ruins and Inca history, he read literature critical of the social and economic marginalization that Indians faced, and he observed the misery and exploitation to which the Inca descendants were subjected. Still, he never seriously considered that their ethnic identity could lead to a type of consciousness that would result in a movement with revolutionary implications.

Particularly in countries with large rural Indigenous populations such as Bolivia and Ecuador, ethnic-based movements have gained a great deal of strength over the last ten to twenty years.[15] Although not organized as guerrilla armies, Indians have been increasingly successful at gaining political space in civil society while still being fundamentally concerned with the same issues of economic inequality and injustice that motivated Che's campaigns. Che maintained in *Guerrilla Warfare* that insurgent groups should not turn to armed struggle until all peaceful means for political change had been exhausted, a point in time that is open to interpretation. Che defined this process primarily in electoral terms. These new ethnic movements, however, have largely eschewed electoral politics in favor of using strikes, marches, and other tools of direct action that the urban Marxist Left had perfected some fifty years earlier. As James Petras has observed, it is within these rural-based movements that the largest potential for revolutionary action currently exists in Latin America.[16]

A primary example of this trend is in Chiapas, Mexico, where the Zapatista guerrillas' dramatic armed uprising on New Year's Day 1994 grabbed international attention.[17] In a sense, this insurrection synthesized many of the issues related to guerrilla warfare as they have developed since the triumph of the Cuban Revolution. Except for the symbolic representation of their media-savvy, urban-raised international spokesperson Subcomandante Marcos (himself almost a legendary Che-type figure), this was undisputably a locally grown revolt. It met all of the primary conditions that Che laid out for a successful guerrilla war. Chiapas's mountainous terrain created a type of ground cover that Che would have found ideal for waging a guerrilla war. After centuries of exploitation, the local Maya Indians had attained a high degree of consciousness as to the nature of their political situation and the necessity for change. As a result, most of the guerrillas were from that area and thus had extensive and immediate knowledge of the local human and physical geography. They enjoyed deep support from the local civilian population. Che could not have asked for more ideal conditions.

Although the Zapatista struggle began as a guerrilla battle, they fought for only eleven days before engaging in peace negotiations with the Mexican government. Like other ethnic struggles, their concerns were fundamentally political rather than military and the Zapatistas and their supporters more often engaged in peaceful direct actions, such as marches, than armed engagements. The Zapatista uprising in Mexico adds ethnic dimensions to the guerrilla struggle that are largely missing in Che's ideological constructions. This extends beyond the obvious ethnic Maya dress and language of the majority of the Zapatista combatants. More significant are the conceptual underpinnings of the movement. Specifically, the Zapatistas have championed the demand for land, not only as an economic commodity but as a territorial component of their culture. They seek to gain political space in Mexican society that they can enter with their complete ethnic identities and concerns intact. Their struggle reflects Mexican Revolutionary war hero Emiliano Zapata's slogan *tierra y libertad*, "land and liberty." Through their grounding in a long history of land and ethnic struggles, they stand poised to carry Che's theories of guerrilla warfare into the twenty-first century.

What has not changed in Mexico nor throughout Latin America since Che wrote *Guerrilla Warfare* in 1960 is the political, social, and economic inequalities that gave rise to revolutionary movements for social justice. In fact, many people throughout the hemisphere were worse off in the 1990s than in the 1960s. As long as these fundamental structural inequalities persist, Ernesto "Che" Guevara will continue to live in the hearts and minds of those who pursue a more fair and just social order.

NOTES

1. See Jon Lee Anderson, *Che Guevara: A Revolutionary Life* (New York: Grove, 1997); Jorge G. Castañeda, *Compañero: The Life and Death of Che Guevara* (New York: Alfred A. Knopf, 1997); and Paco

Ignacio Taibo, *Guevara, Also Known As Che* (New York: St. Martin's, 1997).

2. In analyzing publications on Che, Robert J. Scauzillo concluded that Che's martyrdom "has been given more importance than what he accomplished during his lifetime." Scauzillo, "Ernesto 'Che' Guevara: A Research Bibliography," *Latin American Research Review* 5:2 (Summer 1970): 55.

3. Che recounts this trip in his *The Motorcycle Diaries: A Journey around South America* (London: Fourth Estate, 1996).

4. On Gadea's influence, see Hilda Gadea, *Ernesto: A Memoir of Che Guevara* (New York: Doubleday and Company, 1972). For a broader analysis of these types of ideological influences, see Marc Becker, *Mariátegui and Latin American Marxist Theory*, Monographs in International Studies (Athens: Ohio University Center for International Studies, 1993), 74–80.

5. "The Alliance for Progress," in *Che: Selected Works of Ernesto Guevara*, ed. Rolando E. Bonachea and Nelson P. Valdes (Cambridge MA: MIT Press, 1969), 265–96.

6. Che's Bolivian campaign is described in Ernesto Guevara and Mary-Alice Waters, *The Bolivian Diary of Ernesto Che Guevara* (New York: Pathfinder, 1994). Gary Prado Salmón details his role as a Bolivian army captain in the capture of Che in *The Defeat of Che Guevara: Military Response to Guerrilla Challenge in Bolivia* (New York: Praeger, 1990).

7. Harry E. Vanden, *Marxism in National Latin America: José Carlos Maríategui's Thought and Politics* (Boulder: Lynne Rienner, 1986).

8. Fidel Castro, "The Duty of a Revolutionary Is to Make the Revolution," *Fidel Castro Speaks* (New York: Grove, 1969), 115.

9. Karl Marx and Friedrich Engels, "The Communist Manifesto," in *Karl Marx: Selected Writings*, ed. David McLellan (Oxford: Oxford University Press, 1977), 229.

10. Karl Marx, "The Eighteenth Brumaire of Louis Bonaparte," in *Karl Marx*, 317.

11. Eric R. Wolf, *Peasant Wars of the Twentieth Century* (New York: Harper & Row, 1969).

12. Héctor Béjar, *Peru 1965: Notes on a Guerrilla Experience* (New York: Monthly Review, 1970).

13. For a good summary of these criticisms, see Matt D. Childs, "An Historical Critique of the Emergence and Evolution of Ernesto Che Guevara's *Foco* Theory," *Journal of Latin American studies* 27, 3 (October 1995): 593–624.

14. Sidney W. Mintz, "The Rural Proletariat and the Problem of Rural Proletarian Consciousness," *The Journal of Peasant Studies* 1, 3

(April 1974): 291–325. Che briefly addresses this issue in "Cuba: Exceptional Case or Vanguard," in *Che: Selected Works*, 60.

15. For a summary of this history see Xavier Albó, "El retorno del Indio," *Revista Andina* 9, 2 (December 1991): 299–345.

16. James Petras, "Latin America: The Resurgence of the Left," *New Left Review* 223 (May/June 1997): 17–47.

17. On the Zapatistas, see George Allen Collier and Elizabeth Lowery Quaratiello, *Basta! Land and the Zapatista Rebellion in Chiapas* (Oakland CA: Food First Book, Institute for Food and Development Policy, 1994); Elaine Katzenberger, ed., *First World, Ha Ha Ha! The Zapatista Challenge* (San Francisco: City Lights Books, 1995); and John Ross, *Rebellion from the Roots: Indian Uprising in Chiapas* (Monroe, ME: Common Courage, 1995).

CONTENTS

GUERRILLA WARFARE (1960)

DEDICATION TO CAMILO

The author would like to claim for this work the approval of Camilo Cienfuegos, who was to have read and corrected it when another destiny intervened.[1] These lines and those which follow may be considered the homage of the Rebel Army to its grand captain, to the greatest guerrilla chief that this revolution produced, to a perfect revolutionary and a fraternal friend. Camilo was the companion of a hundred battles, the intimate counselor of Fidel in difficult moments of the war, the stoic fighter who always made of sacrifice an instrument for steeling his own character and forging the morale of his troops. I believe he would have approved of this manual wherein our guerrilla experiences are synthesized, because it is the product of life itself. But he added to the skeleton of words here presented the inner vitality of his temperament, his intelligence and his audacity, all these in such an exact measure as rarely appears in persons of history.

But Camilo should not be seen as an isolated hero performing marvelous feats only on the impulse of his individual genius, but rather as a true part of the peo-

[1] Camilo Cienfuegos was lost at sea during an airplane flight from Camaguey to Havana on October 28, 1959.

ple that formed him, as it always forms its heroes, martyrs, and leaders, by selection in a rigorous struggle.

I do not know if Camilo had heard of Danton's maxim for revolutionary movements, "Audacity, audacity, and more audacity." At any rate, he practiced it in his action and added to it other qualities necessary in a guerrilla fighter: a faculty for precise and rapid analysis of situations and forehanded thought about problems to be resolved in the future.

These lines, which serve as the homage of the author and of a whole people to our hero, will not attempt to provide his biography or even to relate any anecdotes about him. Camilo was the subject of a thousand anecdotes; he created them naturally wherever he went. To his ease of manner, always appreciated by the people, he added a personality that naturally and almost unconsciously put the stamp of Camilo on everything connected with him. Few men have succeeded in leaving on every action such a distinctive personal mark. As Fidel has said, he did not have culture from books; he had the natural intelligence of the people who had chosen him out of thousands for a privileged position on account of the audacity of his blows, his tenacity, intelligence, and unequaled devotion. Camilo practiced loyalty like a religion; he was its votary, both in his personal loyalty to Fidel, who embodied as no one else the will of the people, and in his loyalty to the people themselves. The people and Fidel march united; and thus joined were the devotions of the invincible guerrilla fighter.

Who killed him?

We should rather ask: Who destroyed his body? Because men like him continue to live with the people. Their life does not end so long as the people do not will it.

The enemy succeeded in killing him, because there are no safe airplanes; because pilots cannot acquire all the experience necessary; because, overburdened with work, Camilo wished to be in Havana quickly. His own character killed him, too. Camilo did not measure danger; he used it for a diversion, mocked it, lured, toyed, and played with it. In his mentality as guerrilla fighter a plan was not to be postponed on account of a cloud.

It happened after a whole people had come to know him, admire him, and love him. It could have happened earlier, and his history would be the simple one of a guerrilla captain. "There will be many Camilos," said Fidel; and I can add, there were Camilos, Camilos who finished their lives before completing the magnificent circle that carried Camilo into history. Camilo and the other Camilos (those who did not arrive and those who will come) are the index of the forces of the people. They are the highest expression which a nation produces in a time of war for the defense of its purest ideals, fought with faith in the achievement of its noblest ends.

Let us not try to classify him, to capture him in a mold, that is, kill him. Let us leave him thus, in general lines, without attributing to him a precise social and economic ideology which he never completely defined. Let us emphasize that there was not a soldier to be compared to Camilo in this war of liberation. A thorough revolutionary, a man of the people, a product of this revolution that the Cuban nation made for itself, through his head never passed the lightest shadow of weariness or discouragement. Camilo, the guerrilla warrior, who made this or that thing "something of Camilo," who put his precise and indelible mark on the Cuban Revolution, is a permanent and daily inspiration. He belongs to those others who did not arrive and to those who are to come.

In his continual and immortal renewal, Camilo is the monument of the people.

CHAPTER I

GENERAL PRINCIPLES OF GUERRILLA WARFARE

1. ESSENCE OF GUERRILLA WARFARE

The armed victory of the Cuban people over the Batista dictatorship was not only the triumph of heroism as reported by the newspapers of the world; it also forced a change in the old dogmas concerning the conduct of the popular masses of Latin America. It showed plainly the capacity of the people to free themselves by means of guerrilla warfare from a government that oppresses them.

We consider that the Cuban Revolution contributed three fundamental lessons to the conduct of revolutionary movements in America. They are:

(1) Popular forces can win a war against the army.

(2) It is not necessary to wait until all conditions for making revolution exist; the insurrection can create them.

(3) In underdeveloped America the countryside is the basic area for armed fighting.

Of these three propositions the first two contradict the defeatist attitude of revolutionaries or pseudo-revolutionaries who remain inactive and take refuge in the pretext that against a professional army nothing can be done, who sit down to wait until in some mechanical way all necessary objective and subjective conditions are given without working to accelerate them. As these problems were formerly a subject of discussion in Cuba, until facts settled the question, they are probably still much discussed in America.

Naturally, it is not to be thought that all conditions for revolution are going to be created through the impulse given to them by guerrilla activity. It must always be kept in mind that there is a necessary minimum without which the establishment and consolidation of the first center is not practicable. People must see clearly the futility of maintaining the fight for social goals within the framework of civil debate. When the forces of oppression come to maintain themselves in power against established law, peace is considered already broken.

In these conditions popular discontent expresses itself in more active forms. An attitude of resistance finally crystallizes in an outbreak of fighting, provoked initially by the conduct of the authorities.

Where a government has come into power through some form of popular vote, fraudulent or not, and maintains at least an appearance of constitutional legality, the guerrilla outbreak cannot be promoted, since the possibilities of peaceful struggle have not yet been exhausted.

The third proposition is a fundamental of strategy. It ought to be noted by those who maintain dogmatically that the struggle of the masses is centered in city movements, entirely forgetting the immense participation of the country people in the life of all the underdeveloped parts of America. Of course the struggles of the city masses of organized workers should not be underrated; but their real possibilities of engaging in armed struggle must be carefully analyzed where the guarantees which customarily adorn our constitutions are suspended or ignored. In these conditions the illegal workers' movements face enormous dangers. They must function secretly without arms. The situation in the open country is not so difficult. There, in places beyond the reach of the repressive forces, the inhabitants can be supported by the armed guerrillas.

We will later make a careful analysis of these three conclusions that stand out in the Cuban revolutionary experience. We emphasize them now at the beginning of this work as our fundamental contribution.

Guerrilla warfare, the basis of the struggle of a people to redeem itself, has diverse characteristics, different facets, even though the essential will for liberation remains the same. It is obvious—and writers on the theme have said it many times—that war responds to a certain series of scientific laws; whoever ignores them will go down to defeat. Guerrilla warfare as a phase of war must be ruled by all of these; but besides, because of its special aspects, a series of corollary laws must also be recognized in order to carry it forward. Though geographical and social conditions in each country determine the mode and particular forms that guerrilla warfare will take, there are general laws that hold for all fighting of this type.

Our task at the moment is to find the basic principles of this kind of fighting and the rules to be followed by peoples seeking liberation; to develop theory from facts; to generalize and give structure to our experience for the profit of others.

Let us first consider the question: who are the combatants in guerrilla warfare? On one side we have a group composed of the oppressor and his agents, the professional army, well armed and disciplined, in many cases receiving foreign help as well as the help of the bureaucracy in the employ of the oppressor. On the other side are the people of the nation or region involved. It is important to emphasize that guerrilla warfare is a war of the masses, a war of the people. The guerrilla band is an armed nucleus, the fighting vanguard of the people. It draws its great force from the mass of the people themselves. The guerrilla band is not to be considered inferior to the army against which it fights simply because it is inferior in fire power. Guerrilla warfare is used by the side which is supported by a majority but which possesses a much smaller number of arms for use in defense against oppression.

The guerrilla fighter needs full help from the people of the area. This is an indispensable condition. This is clearly seen by considering the case of bandit gangs that operate in a region. They have all the characteristics of a guerrilla army, homogeneity, respect for the leader, valor, knowledge of the ground, and, often, even good understanding of the tactics to be employed. The only thing missing is support of the people; and, inevitably, these gangs are captured and exterminated by the public force.

Analyzing the mode of operation of the guerrilla band, seeing its form of struggle and understanding its base in the masses, we can answer the question: why does the guerrilla fighter fight? We must come to the inevitable conclusion that the guerrilla fighter is a social reformer, that he takes up arms responding to the angry protest of the people against their oppressors, and that he fights in order to change the social system that keeps all his unarmed brothers in ignominy and misery. He launches himself against the conditions of the reigning institutions at a particular moment and dedicates himself with all the vigor that circumstances permit to breaking the mold of these institutions.

When we analyze more fully the tactic of guerrilla warfare, we will see that the guerrilla fighter needs to have a good knowledge of the surrounding countryside, the paths of entry and escape, the possibilities of speedy maneuver, good hiding places; naturally also, he must count on the support of the people. All this indicates that the guerrilla fighter will carry out his action in wild places of small population. Since in these places the struggle of the people for reforms is aimed primarily and almost exclusively at changing the social form of land ownership, the guerrilla fighter is above all an agrarian revolutionary. He interprets the desires of the great peasant mass to be owners of land, owners of their means of production, of their animals, of all that which they have long yearned to call their own, of that which constitutes their life and will also serve as their cemetery.

It should be noted that in current interpretations there are two different types of guerrilla warfare, one of which—a struggle complementing great regular armies such as was the case of the Ukrainian fighters in the Soviet Union—does not enter into this analysis. We are interested in the other type, the case of an armed group engaged in struggle against the constituted power, whether colonial or not, which establishes itself as the only base and which builds itself up in rural areas. In all such cases, whatever the ideological aims that may inspire the fight, the economic aim is determined by the aspiration toward ownership of land.

The China of Mao begins as an outbreak of worker groups in the South, which is defeated and almost annihilated. It succeeds in establishing itself and begins its advance only when, after the long march from Yenan, it takes up its base in rural territories and makes agrarian reform its fundamental goal. The struggle of Ho Chi Minh is based in the rice-growing peasants, who are oppressed by the French colonial yoke; with this force it is going forward to the defeat of the colonialists. In both cases there is a framework of patriotic war against the Japanese invader, but the economic basis of a fight for the land has not disappeared. In the case of Algeria, the grand idea of Arab nationalism has its economic counterpart in the fact that nearly all of the arable land of Algeria is utilized by a million French settlers. In some countries, such as Puerto Rico, where the special conditions of the island have not permitted a guerrilla outbreak, the nationalist spirit, deeply wounded by the discrimination that is daily practiced, has as its basis the aspiration of the peasants (even though many of them are already a proletariat) to recover the land that the Yankee invader seized from them. This same central idea, though in different forms, inspired the small farmers, peasants, and slaves of the eastern estates of Cuba to close ranks and defend together the right to possess land during the thirty-year war of liberation.[2]

Taking account of the possibilities of development of guerrilla warfare, which is transformed with the increase in the operating potential of the guerrilla band into a war of positions, this type of warfare, despite its special character, is to be considered as an embryo, a prelude, of the other. The possibilities of growth of the guerrilla band and of changes in the mode of fight until conventional warfare is reached, are as great as the possibilities of defeating the enemy in each of the different battles, combats, or skirmishes that take place. Therefore, the fundamental principle is that no battle, combat, or skirmish is to be fought unless it will be won. There is a malevolent definition that says: "The guerrilla fighter is the Jesuit of warfare." By this is indicated a quality of secretiveness, of treachery, of surprise that is obviously an essential element of guerrilla warfare. It is a special kind of Jesuitism, naturally prompted by circumstances, which necessitates acting at certain moments in ways different from the romantic and sporting conceptions with which we are taught to believe war is fought.

[2] The war fought by Cubans for independence from Spain began in 1868 and ended in 1898, with a period of peace from 1878 to 1895.

War is always a struggle in which each contender tries to annihilate the other. Besides using force, they will have recourse to all possible tricks and stratagems in order to achieve the goal. Military strategy and tactics are a representation by analysis of the objectives of the groups and of the means of achieving these objectives. These means contemplate taking advantage of all the weak points of the enemy. The fighting action of each individual platoon in a large army in a war of positions will present the same characteristics as those of the guerrilla band. It uses secretiveness, treachery, and surprise; and when these are not present, it is because vigilance on the other side prevents surprise. But since the guerrilla band is a division unto itself, and since there are large zones of territory not controlled by the enemy, it is always possible to carry out guerrilla attacks in such a way as to assure surprise; and it is the duty of the guerrilla fighter to do so.

"Hit and run" some call this scornfully, and this is accurate. Hit and run, wait, lie in ambush, again hit and run, and thus repeatedly, without giving any rest to the enemy. There is in all this, it would appear, a negative quality, an attitude of retreat, of avoiding frontal fights. However, this is consequent upon the general strategy of guerrilla warfare, which is the same in its ultimate end as is any warfare: to win, to annihilate the enemy.

Thus it is clear that guerrilla warfare is a phase that does not afford in itself opportunities to arrive at complete victory. It is one of the initial phases of warfare and will develop continuously until the guerrilla army in its steady growth acquires the characteristics of a regular army. At that moment it will be ready to deal final blows to the enemy and to achieve victory. Triumph will always be the product of a regular army, even though its origins are in a guerrilla army.

Just as the general of a division in a modern war

does not have to die in front of his soldiers, the guerrilla fighter, who is general of himself, need not die in every battle. He is ready to give his life, but the positive quality of this guerrilla warfare is precisely that each one of the guerrilla fighters is ready to die, not to defend an ideal, but rather to convert it into reality. This is the basis, the essence of guerrilla fighting. Miraculously, a small band of men, the armed vanguard of the great popular force that supports them, goes beyond the immediate tactical objective, goes on decisively to achieve an ideal, to establish a new society, to break the old molds of the outdated, and to achieve, finally, the social justice for which they fight.

Considered thus, all these disparaged qualities acquire a true nobility, the nobility of the end at which they aim; and it becomes clear that we are not speaking of distorted means of reaching an end. This fighting attitude, this attitude of not being dismayed at any time, this inflexibility when confronting the great problems in the final objective is also the nobility of the guerrilla fighter.

2. GUERRILLA STRATEGY

In guerrilla terminology, strategy is understood as the analysis of the objectives to be achieved in the light of the total military situation and the overall ways of reaching these objectives.

To have a correct strategic appreciation from the point of view of the guerrilla band, it is necessary to analyze fundamentally what will be the enemy's mode of action. If the final objective is always the complete destruction of the opposite force, the enemy is confronted in the case of a civil war of this kind with the standard task: he will have to achieve the total destruction of each one of the components of the guerrilla band. The guerrilla fighter, on the other hand, must analyze the resources which the enemy has for trying to achieve that outcome: the means in men, in mobility, in popular support, in armaments, in capacity of leadership on which he can count. We must make our own strategy adequate on the basis of these studies, keeping in mind always the final objective of defeating the enemy army.

There are fundamental aspects to be studied: the armament, for example, and the manner of using this armament. The value of a tank, of an airplane in a fight of this type must be weighed. The arms of the enemy, his ammunition, his habits must be considdered; because the principal source of provision for the guerrilla force is precisely in enemy armaments. If there is a possibility of choice, we should prefer the same type as that used by the enemy, since the greatest problem of the guerrilla band is the lack of ammunition, which the opponent must provide.

After the objectives have been fixed and analyzed, it is necessary to study the order of the steps leading to the achievement of the final objective. This should be planned in advance, even though it will be modified and adjusted as the fighting develops and unforeseen circumstances arise.

At the outset, the essential task of the guerrilla fighter is to keep himself from being destroyed. Little by little it will be easier for the members of the guerrilla band or bands to adapt themselves to their form of life and to make flight and escape from the forces that are on the offensive an easy task, because it is performed daily. When this condition is reached, the guerrilla, having taken up inaccessible positions out of reach of the enemy, or having assembled forces that deter the enemy from attacking, ought to proceed to the gradual weakening of the enemy. This will be carried out at first at those points nearest to the points of active warfare against the guerrilla band

and later will be taken deeper into enemy territory, attacking his communications, later attacking or harassing his bases of operations and his central bases, tormenting him on all sides to the full extent of the capabilities of the guerrilla forces.

The blows should be continuous. The enemy soldier in a zone of operations ought not to be allowed to sleep; his outposts ought to be attacked and liquidated systematically. At every moment the impression ought to be created that he is surrounded by a complete circle. In wooded and broken areas this effort should be maintained both day and night; in open zones that are easily penetrated by enemy patrols, at night only. In order to do all this the absolute cooperation of the people and a perfect knowledge of the ground is necessary. These two necessities affect every minute of the life of the guerrilla fighter. Therefore, along with centers for study of present and future zones of operations, intensive popular work must be undertaken to explain the motives of the revolution, its ends, and to spread the incontrovertible truth that victory of the enemy against the people is finally impossible. *Whoever does not feel this undoubted truth cannot be a guerrilla fighter.*

This popular work should at first be aimed at securing secrecy; that is, each peasant, each member of the society in which action is taking place, will be asked not to mention what he sees and hears; later, help will be sought from inhabitants whose loyalty to the revolution offers greater guarantees; still later, use will be made of these persons in missions of contact, for transporting goods or arms, as guides in the zones familiar to them; still later, it is possible to arrive at organized mass action in the centers of work, of which the final result will be the general strike.

The strike is a most important factor in civil war, but in order to reach it a series of complementary conditions are necessary which do not always exist and which very rarely come to exist spontaneously. It is necessary to create these essential conditions, basically by explaining the purposes of the revolution and by demonstrating the forces of the people and their possibilities.

It is also possible to have recourse to certain very homogeneous groups, which must have shown their efficacy previously in less dangerous tasks, in order to make use of another of the terrible arms of the guerrilla band, sabotage. It is possible to paralyze entire armies, to suspend the industrial life of a zone, leaving the inhabitants of a city without factories, without light, without water, without communications of any kind, without being able to risk travel by highway except at certain hours. If all this is achieved, the morale of the enemy falls, the morale of his combatant units weakens, and the fruit ripens for plucking at a precise moment.

All this presupposes an increase in the territory included within the guerrilla action, but an excessive increase of this territory is to be avoided. It is essential always to preserve a strong base of operations and to continue strengthening it during the course of the war. Within this territory, measures of indoctrination of the inhabitants of the zone should be utilized; measures of quarantine should be taken against the irreconcilable enemies of the revolution; all the purely defensive measures, such as trenches, mines, and communications, should be perfected.

When the guerrilla band has reached a respectable power in arms and in number of combatants, it ought to proceed to the formation of new columns. This is an act similar to that of the beehive when at a given moment it releases a new queen, who goes to another region with a part of the swarm. The mother hive with the most notable guerrilla chief will stay in the less dangerous places, while the new columns will penetrate other enemy territories following the cycle already described.

A moment will arrive in which the territory occupied by the columns is too small for them; and in the advance toward regions solidly defended by the enemy, it will be necessary to confront powerful forces. At that instant the columns join, they offer a compact fighting front, and a war of positions is reached, a war carried on by regular armies. However, the former guerrilla army cannot cut itself off from its base, and it should create new guerrilla bands behind the enemy acting in the same way as the original bands operated earlier, proceeding thus to penetrate enemy territory until it is dominated.

It is thus that guerrillas reach the stage of attack, of the encirclement of fortified bases, of the defeat of reinforcements, of mass action, ever more ardent, in the whole national territory, arriving finally at the objective of the war: victory.

3. GUERRILLA TACTICS

In military language, tactics are the practical methods of achieving the grand strategic objectives.

In one sense they complement strategy and in another they are more specific rules within it. As means, tactics are much more variable, much more flexible than the final objectives, and they should be adjusted continually during the struggle. There are tactical objectives that remain constant throughout a war and others that vary. The first thing to be considered is the adjusting of guerrilla action to the action of the enemy.

The fundamental characteristic of a guerrilla band is mobility. This permits it in a few minutes to move far from a specific theatre and in a few hours far even from the region, if that becomes necessary; permits it constantly to change front and avoid any type of encirclement. As the circumstances of the war require, the guerrilla band can dedicate itself exclusively to fleeing from an encirclement which is the enemy's only way of forcing the band into a decisive fight that could be unfavorable; it can also change the battle into a counter-encirclement (small bands of men are presumably surrounded by the enemy when suddenly the enemy is surrounded by stronger contingents; or men located in a safe place serve as a lure, leading to the encirclement and annihilation of the entire troops and supply of an attacking force). Characteristic of this war of mobility is the so-called minuet, named from the analogy with the dance: the guerrilla bands encircle an enemy position, an advancing column, for example; they encircle it completely from the four points of the compass, with five or six men in each place, far enough away to avoid being encircled themselves; the fight is started at any one of the points, and the army moves toward it; the guerrilla band then retreats, always maintaining visual contact, and initiates its attack from another point. The army will repeat its action and the guerrilla band the same. Thus, successively, it is possible to keep an enemy column immobilized, forcing it to expend large quantities of ammunition and weakening the morale of its troops without incurring great dangers.

This same tactic can be applied at nighttime, closing in more and showing greater aggressiveness, because in these conditions counter-encirclement is much more difficult. Movement by night is another important characteristic of the guerrilla band, enabling it to advance into position for an attack and, where the danger of betrayal exists, to mobilize in new territory. The numerical inferiority of the guerrilla makes it necessary that attacks always be carried out by surprise; this great advantage is what permits the guerrilla fighter to inflict losses on the enemy without suffering losses. In a fight between a hundred men on one side and ten on the other, losses are not equal where there is one casualty on each side. The enemy loss is always reparable; it amounts to only one percent of his effectives. The loss of the guerrilla band requires more time to be repaired because it involves a soldier of high specialization and is ten percent of the operating forces.

A dead soldier of the guerrillas ought never to be left with his arms and his ammunition. The duty of every guerrilla soldier whenever a companion falls is to recover immediately these extremely precious elements of the fight. In fact, the care which must be taken of ammunition and the method of using it are further characteristics of guerrilla warfare. In any combat between a regular force and a guerrilla band it is always possible to know one from the other by their different manner of fire: a great amount of firing on the part of the regular army, sporadic and accurate shots on the part of the guerrillas.

Once one of our heroes, now dead, had to employ his machine guns for nearly five minutes, burst after burst, in order to slow up the advance of enemy soldiers. This fact caused considerable confusion in our forces, because they assumed from the rhythm of fire that that key position must have been taken by the enemy, since this was one of the rare occasions where departure from the rule of saving fire had been called for because of the importance of the point being defended.

Another fundamental characteristic of the guerrilla soldier is his flexibility, his ability to adapt himself to all circumstances, and to convert to his service all of the accidents of the action. Against the rigidity of classical methods of fighting, the guerrilla fighter invents his own tactics at every minute of the fight and constantly surprises the enemy.

In the first place, there are only elastic positions, specific places that the enemy cannot pass, and places of diverting him. Frequently the enemy, after easily overcoming difficulties in a gradual advance, is surprised to find himself suddenly and solidly detained without possibilities of moving forward. This is due to the fact that the guerrilla-defended positions, when they have been selected on the basis of a careful study of the ground, are invulnerable. It is not the number of attacking soldiers that counts, but the number of defending soldiers. Once that number has been placed there, it can nearly always hold off a battalion with success. It is a major task of the chiefs to choose well the moment and the place for defending a position without retreat.

The form of attack of a guerrilla army is also different; starting with surprise and fury, irresistible, it suddenly converts itself into total passivity.

The surviving enemy, resting, believes that the attacker has departed; he begins to relax, to return to the routine life of the camp or of the fortress, when suddenly a new attack bursts forth in another place, with the same characteristics, while the main body of the guerrilla band lies in wait to intercept reinforcements. At other times an outpost defending the camp will be suddenly attacked by the guerrilla, dominated, and captured. The fundamental thing is surprise and rapidity of attack.

Acts of sabotage are very important. It is necessary to distinguish clearly between sabotage, a revolutionary and highly effective method of warfare, and terrorism, a measure that is generally ineffective and indiscriminate in its results, since it often makes victims of innocent people and destroys a large number of lives that would be valuable to the revolution. Terrorism should be considered a valuable tactic when it is used to put to death some noted leader of the oppressing forces well known for his cruelty, his efficiency in repression, or other quality that makes his elimination useful. But the killing of persons of small importance is never advisable, since it brings on an increase of reprisals, including deaths.

There is one point very much in controversy in opinions about terrorism. Many consider that its use, by provoking police oppression, hinders all more or less legal or semiclandestine contact with the masses and makes impossible unification for actions that will be necessary at a critical moment. This is correct; but it also happens that in a civil war the repression by the governmental power in certain towns is already so great that, in fact, every type of legal action is suppressed already, and any action of the masses that is not supported by arms is impossible. It is therefore necessary to be circumspect in adopting methods of this type and to consider the consequences that they may bring for the revolution. At any rate, well-managed sabotage is always a very effective arm, though it should not be employed to put means of production out of action, leaving a sector of the population paralyzed (and thus without work) unless this paralysis affects the normal life of the society. It is ridiculous to carry out sabotage against a soft-drink factory, but it is absolutely correct and advisable to carry out sabotage against a power plant. In the first case, a certain number of workers are put out of a job but nothing is done to modify the rhythm of industrial life; in the second case, there will again be displaced workers, but this is entirely justified by the paralysis of the life of the region. We will return to the technique of sabotage later.

One of the favorite arms of the enemy army, supposed to be decisive in modern times, is aviation. Nevertheless, this has no use whatsoever during the period that guerrilla warfare is in its first stages, with small concentrations of men in rugged places. The utility of aviation lies in the systematic destruction of visible and organized defenses; and for this there must be large concentrations of men who construct these defenses, something that does not exist in this type of warfare. Planes are also potent against marches by columns through level places or places without cover; however, this latter danger is easily avoided by carrying out the marches at night.

One of the weakest points of the enemy is transportation by road and railroad. It is virtually impossible to maintain a vigil yard by yard over a transport line, a road, or a railroad. At any point a considerable amount of explosive charge can be planted that will make the road impassable; or by exploding it at the moment that a vehicle passes, a considerable loss in lives and materiel to the enemy is caused at the same time that the road is cut.

The sources of explosives are varied. They can be brought from other zones; or use can be made of bombs seized from the dictatorship, though these do not always work; or they can be manufactured in secret laboratories within the guerrilla zone. The technique of setting them off is quite varied; their manufacture also depends upon the conditions of the guerrilla band.

In our laboratory we made powder which we used as a cap, and we invented various devices for exploding the mines at the desired moment. The ones that gave the best results were electric. The first mine that we exploded was a bomb dropped from an aircraft of the dictatorship. We adapted it by inserting various caps and adding a gun with the trigger pulled by a cord. At the moment that an enemy truck passed, the weapon was fired to set off the explosion.

These techniques can be developed to a high degree. We have information that in Algeria, for example, tele-explosive mines, that is, mines exploded by radio at great distances from the point where they are located, are being used today against the French colonial power.

The technique of lying in ambush along roads in order to explode mines and annihilate survivors is one of the most remunerative in point of ammunition and arms. The surprised enemy does not use his ammunition and has no time to flee; so with a small expenditure of ammunition large results are achieved.

As blows are dealt the enemy, he also changes his tactics, and in place of isolated trucks, veritable motorized columns move. However, by choosing the ground well, the same result can be produced by breaking the column and concentrating forces on one vehicle. In these cases the essential elements of guerrilla tactics must always be kept in mind. These are: perfect knowledge of the ground; surveillance and foresight as to the lines of escape; vigilance over all the secondary roads that can bring support to the point of attack; intimacy with people in the zone so as to have sure help from them in respect to supplies, transport, and temporary or permanent hiding places if it becomes necessary to leave wounded companions behind; numerical superiority at a chosen point of action; total mobility; and the possibility of counting on reserves.

If all these tactical requisites are fulfilled, surprise attack along the lines of communication of the enemy yields notable dividends.

A fundamental part of guerrilla tactics is the treatment accorded the people of the zone. Even the treatment accorded the enemy is important; the norm to be followed should be an absolute inflexibility at the time of attack, an absolute inflexibility toward all the despicable elements that resort to informing and assassination, and clemency as absolute as possible toward the enemy soldiers who go into the fight performing or believing that they perform a military duty. It is a good policy, so long as there are no considerable bases of operations and invulnerable places, to take no prisoners. Survivors ought to be set free. The wounded should be cared for with all possible resources at the time of the action. Conduct toward the civil population ought to be regulated by a large respect for all the rules and traditions of the people of the zone, in order to demonstrate effectively, with deeds, the moral superiority of the guerrilla fighter over the oppressing soldier. Except in special situations, there ought to be no execution of justice without giving the criminal an opportunity to clear himself.

4. WARFARE ON FAVORABLE GROUND

As we have already said, guerrilla fighting will not always take place in country most favorable to the employment of its tactics; but when it does, that is, when the guerrilla band is located in zones difficult to reach, either because of dense forests, steep mountains, impassable deserts or marshes, the general tactics, based on the fundamental postulates of guerrilla warfare, must always be the same.

An important point to consider is the moment for making contact with the enemy. If the zone is so thick, so difficult that an organized army can never reach it, the guerrilla band should advance to the regions where the army can arrive and where there will be a possibility of combat.

As soon as the survival of the guerrilla band has been assured, it should fight; it must constantly go out from its refuge to fight. Its mobility does not have to be as great as in those cases where the ground is unfavorable; it must adjust itself to the capabilities of the enemy, but it is not necessary to be able to move as quickly as in places where the enemy can concentrate a large number of men in a few minutes. Neither is the nocturnal character of this warfare so important; it will be possible in many cases to carry out daytime operations, especially mobilizations by day, though subjected to enemy observation by land and air. It is also possible to persist in a military action for a much longer time, above all in the mountains; it is possible to undertake battles of long duration with very few men, and it is very probable that the arrival of enemy reinforcements at the scene of the fight can be prevented.

A close watch over the points of access is, however, an axiom never to be forgotten by the guerrilla fighter. His aggressiveness (on account of the difficulties that the enemy faces in bringing up reinforcements) can be greater, he can approach the enemy more closely, fight much more directly, more frontally and for a longer time, though these rules may be qualified by various circumstances, such, for example, as the amount of ammunition.

Fighting on favorable ground and particularly in the mountains presents many advantages but also the inconvenience that it is difficult to capture in a single operation a considerable quantity of arms and ammunition, owing to the precautions that the enemy takes in these regions. (The guerrilla soldier must never forget the fact that it is the enemy that must serve as his source of supply of ammunition and arms.) But much more rapidly than in unfavorable ground the guerrilla band will here be able to "dig in," that is, to form a base capable of engaging in a war of positions, where small industries may be installed as they are needed, as well as hospitals, centers for education and training, storage facilities, organs of propaganda, etc., adequately protected from aviation or from long-range artillery.

The guerrilla band in these conditions can number

many more personnel; there will be noncombatants and perhaps even a system of training in the use of the arms that eventually are to fall into the power of the guerrilla army.

The number of men that a guerrilla band can have is a matter of extremely flexible calculation adapted to the territory, to the means available of acquiring supplies, to the mass flights of oppressed people from other zones, to the arms available, to the necessities of organization. But, in any case, it is much more practicable to establish a base and expand with the support of new combatant elements.

The radius of action of a guerrilla band of this type can be as wide as conditions or the operations of other bands in adjacent territory permit. The range will be limited by the time that it takes to arrive at a zone of security from the zone of operation; assuming that marches must be made at night, it will not be possible to operate more than five or six hours away from a point of maximum security. Small guerrilla bands that work constantly at weakening a territory can go farther away from the zone of security.

The arms preferable for this type of warfare are long-range weapons requiring small expenditure of bullets, supported by a group of automatic or semi-automatic arms. Of the rifles and machine guns that exist in the markets of the United States, one of the best is the M-1 rifle, called the Garand. However, this should be used only by people with some experience, since it has the disadvantage of expending too much ammunition. Medium-heavy arms, such as tripod machine guns, can be used on favorable ground, affording a greater margin of security for the weapon and its personnel, but they ought always to be a means of repelling an enemy and not for attack.

An ideal composition for a guerrilla band of 25 men would be: 10 to 15 single-shot rifles and about 10 automatic arms between Garands and hand machine guns, including light and easily portable automatic arms, such as the Browning or the more modern Belgian FAL and M-14 automatic rifles. Among the hand machine guns the best are those of nine millimeters, which permit a larger transport of ammunition. The simpler its construction the better, because this increases the ease of switching parts. All this must be adjusted to the armament that the enemy uses, since the ammunition that he employs is what we are going to use when his arms fall into our hands. It is practically impossible for heavy arms to be used. Aircraft cannot see anything and cease to operate; tanks and cannons cannot do much owing to the difficulties of advancing in these zones.

A very important consideration is supply. In general, the zones of difficult access for this very reason present special problems, since there are few peasants, and therefore animal and food supplies are scarce. It is necessary to maintain stable lines of communication in order to be able always to count on a minimum of food, stockpiled, in the event of any disagreeable development.

In this kind of zone of operations the possibilities of sabotage on a large scale are generally not present; with the inaccessibility goes a lack of constructions, telephone lines, aqueducts, etc., that could be damaged by direct action.

For supply purposes it is important to have animals, among which the mule is the best in rough country. Adequate pasturage permitting good nutrition is essential. The mule can pass through extremely hilly country impossible for other animals. In the most difficult situations it is necessary to resort to transport by men. Each individual can carry twenty-five kilograms for many hours daily and for many days.

The lines of communication with the exterior should include a series of intermediate points manned by people of complete reliability, where products can be stored and where contacts can go to hide themselves at critical times. Internal lines of communication can also be created. Their extension will be determined by the stage of development reached by the guerrilla band. In some zones of operations in the recent Cuban war, telephone lines of many kilometers of length were established, roads were built, and a messenger service maintained sufficient to cover all zones in a minimum of time.

There are also other possible means of communication, not used in the Cuban war but perfectly applicable, such as smoke signals, signals with sunshine reflected by mirrors, and carrier pigeons.

The vital necessities of the guerrillas are to maintain their arms in good condition, to capture ammunition, and, above everything else, to have adequate shoes. The first manufacturing efforts should therefore be directed toward these objectives. Shoe factories can initially be cobbler installations that replace half-soles on old shoes, expanding afterwards into a series of organized factories with a good average daily production of shoes. The manufacture of powder is fairly simple; and much can be accomplished by having a small laboratory and bringing in the necessary materials from outside. Mined areas constitute a grave danger for the enemy; large areas can be mined for simultaneous explosion, destroying up to hundreds of men.

5. WARFARE ON UNFAVORABLE GROUND

In order to carry on warfare in country that is not very hilly, lacks forests, and has many roads, all the fundamental requisites of guerrilla warfare must be observed; only the forms will be altered. The quantity, not the quality, of guerrilla warfare will change. For example, following the same order as before, the mobility of this type of guerrilla should be extraordinary; strikes should be made preferably at night; they should be extremely rapid but the guerrilla should move to places different from the starting point, the farthest possible from the scene of action, assuming that there is no place secure from the repressive forces that the guerrilla can use as its garrison.

A man can walk between 30 and 50 kilometers during the night hours; it is possible also to march during the first hours of daylight, unless the zones of operation are closely watched or there is danger that people in the vicinity, seeing the passing troops, will notify the pursuing army of the location of the guerrilla band and its route. It is always preferable in these cases to operate at night with the greatest possible silence both before and after the action; the first hours of night are best. Here too there are exceptions to the general rule, since at times the dawn hours will be preferable. It is never wise to habituate the enemy to a certain form of warfare; it is necessary to vary constantly the places, the hours, and the forms of operation.

We have already said that the action cannot endure for long, but must be rapid; it must be of a high degree of effectiveness, last a few minutes, and be followed by an immediate withdrawal. The arms employed here will not be the same as in the case of actions on favorable ground; a large quantity of automatic weapons is to be preferred. In night attacks marksmanship is not the determining factor, but rather concentration of fire; the more automatic arms firing at short distance, the more possibilities there are of annihilating the enemy.

Also, the use of mines in roads and the destruction of bridges are tactics of great importance. Attacks by the guerrilla will be less aggressive so far as the persistence and continuation are concerned, but they can be very violent, and they can utilize different arms, such as mines and the shotgun. Against open vehicles heavily loaded with men, which is the usual method of transporting troops, and even against closed vehicles that do not have special defenses—against buses, for example—the shotgun is a tremendous weapon. A shotgun loaded with large shot is the most effective. This is not a secret of guerrilla fighters; it is used also in big wars. The Americans used shotgun platoons armed with high-quality weapons and bayonets for assaulting machine-gun nests.

There is an important problem to explain, that of ammunition; this will almost always be taken from the enemy. It is therefore necessary to strike blows where there will be the absolute assurance of restoring the ammunition expended, unless there are large reserves in secure places. In other words, an annihilating attack against a group of men is not to be undertaken at the risk of expending all ammunition without being able to replace it. Always in guerrilla tactics it is necessary to keep in mind the grave problem of procuring the war materiel necessary for continuing the fight. For this reason guerrilla arms ought to be the same as those used by the enemy, except for weapons such as revolvers and shotguns, for which the ammunition can be obtained in the zone itself or in the cities.

The number of men that a guerrilla band of this type should include does not exceed ten to fifteen. In forming a single combat unit it is of great importance always to consider the limitations on numbers: ten, twelve, fifteen men can hide anywhere and at the same time can help each other in putting up a powerful resistance to the enemy. Four or five would perhaps be too small a number, but when the number exceeds ten the possibility that the enemy will discover them in their camp or on the march is much greater.

Remember that the velocity of the guerrilla band on the march is equal to the velocity of its slowest man. It is more difficult to find uniformity of marching speed with twenty, thirty, or forty men than with ten. And the guerrilla fighter on the plain must be fundamentally a runner. Here the practice of hitting and running acquires its maximum use. The guerrilla bands on the plain suffer the enormous inconvenience of being subject to a rapid encirclement and of not having sure places where they can set up a firm resistance; therefore they must live in conditions of absolute secrecy for a long time, since it would be dangerous to trust any neighbor whose fidelity is not perfectly established. The reprisals of the enemy are so violent, usually so brutal, inflicted not only on the head of the family but frequently on the women and children as well, that pressure on individuals lacking firmness may result at any moment in their giving way and revealing information as to where the guerrilla band is located and how it is operating. This would immediately produce an encirclement with consequences always disagreeable, although not necessarily fatal. When conditions, the quantity of arms, and the state of insurrection of the people call for an increase in the number of men, the guerrilla band should be divided. If it is necessary, all can rejoin at a given moment to deal a blow, but in such a way that immediately afterwards they can disperse toward separate zones, again divided into small groups of ten, twelve, or fifteen men.

It is entirely feasible to organize whole armies under a single command and to assure respect and obedience to this command without the necessity of being in a single group. Therefore the election of the guerrilla chiefs and the certainty that they coordinate ideologically and personally with the overall chief of the zone are very important.

The bazooka is a heavy weapon that can be used by

the guerrilla band because of its easy portability and operation. Today the rifle-fired anti-tank grenade can replace it. Naturally, it will be a weapon taken from the enemy. The bazooka is ideal for firing on armored vehicles, and even on unarmored vehicles that are loaded with troops, and for taking small military bases of few men in a short time; but it is important to point out that not more than three shells per man can be carried, and this only with considerable exertion.

As for the utilization of heavy arms taken from the enemy, naturally nothing is to be scorned. But there are weapons such as the tripod machine gun, the heavy fifty-millimeter machine gun, etc., that, when captured, can be utilized with a willingness to lose them again. In other words, in the unfavorable conditions that we are now analyzing, a battle to defend a heavy machine gun or other weapon of this type cannot be allowed; they are simply to be used until the tactical moment when they must be abandoned. In our Cuban war of liberation, to abandon a weapon constituted a grave offense, and there was never any case where the necessity arose. Nevertheless, we mention this case in order to explain clearly the only situation in which abandonment would not constitute an occcasion for reproaches. On unfavorable ground, the guerrilla weapon is the personal weapon of rapid fire.

Easy access to the zone usually means that it will be habitable and that there will be a peasant population in these places. This facilitates supply enormously. Having trustworthy people and making contact with establishments that provide supplies to the population, it is possible to maintain a guerrilla band perfectly well without having to devote time or money to long and dangerous lines of communication. Also it is well to reiterate that the smaller the number of men the easier it will be to procure food for them. Essential supplies such as bedding, waterproof material, mosquito netting, shoes, medicines, and food will be found directly in the zone, since they are things of daily use by its inhabitants.

Communications will be much easier in the sense of being able to count on a larger number of men and more roads; but they will be more difficult as a problem of security for messages between distant points, since it will be necessary to rely on a series of contacts that have to be trusted. There will be the danger of an eventual capture of one of the messengers, who are constantly crossing enemy zones. If the messages are of small importance, they should be oral; if of great importance, code writing should be used. Experience shows that transmission by word of mouth greatly distorts any communication.

For these same reasons manufacture will have much less importance, at the same time that it would be much more difficult to carry it out. It will not be possible to have factories making shoes or arms. Practically speaking, manufacture will have to be limited to small shops, carefully hidden, where shotgun shells can be recharged and mines, simple grenades, and other minimum necessities of the moment manufactured. On the other hand, it is possible to make use of all the friendly shops of the zone for such work as is necessary.

This brings us to two consequenes that flow logically from what has been said. One of them is that the favorable conditions for establishing a permanent camp in guerrilla warfare are inverse to the degree of productive development of a place. All favorable conditions, all facilities of life normally induce men to settle; but for the guerrilla band the opposite is the case. The more facilities there are for social life, the more nomadic, the more uncertain the life of the guerrilla fighter. These really are the results of one and the same principle. The title of this section is "War on Unfavorable Ground," because everything that is favorable to human life, communications, urban and semi-urban concentrations of large numbers of people, land easily worked by machine, all these place the guerrilla fighter in a disadvantageous situation.

The second conclusion is that if guerrilla fighting must include the extremely important factor of work on the masses, this work is even more important in the unfavorable zones, where a single enemy attack can produce a catastrophe. Indoctrination should be continuous, and so should be the struggle for unity of the workers, of the peasants, and of other social classes that live in the zone, in order to achieve toward the guerrilla fighters a maximum homogeneity of attitude. This task with the masses, this constant work at the huge problem of relations of the guerrilla band with the inhabitants of the zone, must also govern the attitude to be taken toward the case of an individual recalcitrant enemy soldier: he should be eliminated without hesitation when he is dangerous. In this respect the guerrilla band must be drastic. Enemies cannot be permitted to exist within the zone of operations in places that offer no security.

6. SUBURBAN WARFARE

If during the war the guerrilla bands close in on cities and penetrate the surrounding country in such a way as to be able to establish themselves in conditions of some security, it will be necessary to give these suburban bands a special education, or rather, a special organization.

It is fundamental to recognize that a suburban guerrilla band can never spring up of its own accord. It will be born only after certain conditions necessary for its survival have been created. Therefore, the suburban guerrilla will always be under the direct orders of chiefs located in another zone. The function of this guerrilla band will not be to carry out independent actions but to coordinate its activities with overall strategic plans in such a way as to support the action of larger groups situated in another area, contributing specifically to the success of a fixed tactical objective, without the operational freedom of guerrilla bands of the other types. For example, a suburban band will not be able to choose among the operations of destroying telephone lines, moving to make attacks in another locality, and surprising a patrol of soldiers on a distant road; it will do exactly what it is told. If its function is to cut down telephone poles or electric wires, to destroy sewers, railroads, or water mains, it will limit itself to carrying out these tasks efficiently.

It ought not to number more than four or five men. The limitation on numbers is important, because the suburban guerrilla must be considered as situated in exceptionally unfavorable ground, where the vigilance of the enemy will be much greater and the possibilities of reprisals as well as of betrayal are increased enormously. Another aggravating circumstance is that the suburban guerrilla band cannot depart far from the places where it is going to operate. To speed of action and withdrawal there must be added a limitation on the distance of withdrawal from the scene of action and the need to remain totally hidden during the daytime. This is a nocturnal guerrilla band in the extreme, without possibilities of changing its manner of operating until the insurrection is so far advanced that it can take part as an active combatant in the siege of the city.

The essential qualities of the guerrilla fighter in this situation are discipline (perhaps in the highest degree of all) and discretion. He cannot count on more than two or three friendly houses that will provide food; it is almost certain that an encirclement in these conditions will be equivalent to death. Weapons, furthermore, will not be of the same kind as those of the other groups. They will be for personal defense, of the type that do not hinder a rapid flight or betray a secure hiding place. As their armament the band ought to have not more than one carbine or one sawed-off shotgun, or perhaps two, with pistols for the other members.

They will concentrate their action on prescribed sabotage and never carry out armed attacks, except by surprising one or two members or agents of the enemy troops.

For sabotage they need a full set of instruments. The guerrilla fighter must have good saws, large quantities of dynamite, picks and shovels, apparatus for lifting rails, and, in general, adequate mechanical equipment for the work to be carried out. This should be hidden in places that are secure but easily accessible to the hands that will need to use it.

If there is more than one guerrilla band, they will all be under a single chief who will give orders as to the necessary tasks through contacts of proven trustworthiness who live openly as ordinary citizens. In certain cases the guerrilla fighter will be able to maintain his peacetime work, but this is very difficult. Practically speaking, the suburban guerrilla band is a group of men who are already outside the law, in a condition of war, situated as unfavorably as we have described.

The importance of a suburban struggle has usually been underestimated; it is really very great. A good operation of this type extended over a wide area paralyzes almost completely the commercial and industrial life of the sector and places the entire population in a situation of unrest, of anguish, almost of impatience for the development of violent events that will relieve the period of suspense. If from the first moment of the war, thought is taken for the future possibility of this type of fight and an organization of specialists started, a much more rapid action will be assured, and with it a saving of lives and of the priceless time of the nation.

CHAPTER II

THE GUERRILLA BAND

1. THE GUERRILLA FIGHTER: SOCIAL REFORMER

We have already described the guerrilla fighter as one who shares the longing of the people for liberation and who, once peaceful means are exhausted, initiates the fight and converts himself into an armed vanguard of the fighting people. From the very beginning of the struggle he has the intention of destroying an unjust order and therefore an intention, more or less hidden, to replace the old with something new.

We have also already said that in the conditions that prevail, at least in America and in almost all countries with deficient economic development, it is the countryside that offers ideal conditions for the fight. Therefore the foundation of the social structure that the guerrilla fighter will build begins with changes in the ownership of agrarian property.

The banner of the fight throughout this period will be agrarian reform. At first this goal may or may not be completely delineated in its extent and limits; it may simply refer to the age-old hunger of the peasant for the land on which he works or wishes to work.

The conditions in which the agrarian reform will be realized depend upon the conditions which existed before the struggle began, and on the social depth of the struggle. But the guerrilla fighter, as a person conscious of a role in the vanguard of the people, must have a moral conduct that shows him to be a true priest of the reform to which he aspires. To the stoicism imposed by the difficult conditions of warfare should be added an austerity born of rigid self-control that will prevent a single excess, a single slip, whatever the circumstances. The guerrilla soldier should be an ascetic.

As for social relations, these will vary with the development of the war. At the beginning it will not be possible to attempt any changes in the social order.

Merchandise that cannot be paid for in cash will be paid for with bonds; and these should be redeemed at the first opportunity.

The peasant must always be helped technically, economically, morally, and culturally. The guerrilla fighter will be a sort of guiding angel who has fallen into the zone, helping the poor always and bothering the rich as little as possible in the first phases of the war. But this war will continue on its course; contradictions will continuously become sharper; the moment will arive when many of those who regarded the revolution with a certain sympathy at the outset will place themselves in a position diametrically opposed; and they will take the first step into battle against the popular forces. At that moment the guerrilla fighter should act to make himself into the standard bearer of the cause of the people, punishing every betrayal with justice. Private property should acquire in the war zones its social function. For example, excess land and livestock not essential for the maintenance of a wealthy family should pass into the hands of the people and be distributed equitably and justly.

The right of the owners to receive payment for possessions used for the social good ought always to be respected; but this payment will be made in bonds ("bonds of hope," as they were called by our teacher, General Bayo,[3] referring to the common interest that is thereby established between debtor and creditor).

The land and property of notorious and active enemies of the revolution should pass immediately into the hands of the revolutionary forces. Furthermore, taking advantage of the heat of the war—those moments in which human fraternity reaches its highest intensity—all kinds of cooperative work, as much as the mentality of the inhabitants will permit, ought to be stimulated.

The guerrilla fighter as a social reformer should not only provide an example in his own life but he ought also constantly to give orientation in ideological problems, explaining what he knows and what he wishes to do at the right time. He will also make use of what he learns as the months or years of the war strengthen his revolutionary convictions, making him more radical as the potency of arms is demonstrated, as the outlook of the inhabitants becomes a part of his spirit and of his own life, and as he understands the justice and the vital necessity of a series of changes, of which the theoretical importance appeared to him before, but devoid of practical urgency.

This development occurs very often, because the initiators of guerrilla warfare, or rather the directors of guerrilla warfare, are not men who have bent their backs day after day over the furrow. They are men who understand the necessity for changes in the social treatment accorded peasants, without having suffered in the usual case this bitter treatment in their own per-

[3] Colonel Alberto Bayo, a Cuban veteran of guerrilla warfare in Spain, served as instructor of the forces assembled by Fidel Castro in Mexico for training prior to the invasion of Cuba in December 1956.

sons. It happens then (I am drawing on the Cuban experience and enlarging it) that a genuine interaction is produced between these leaders, who with their acts teach the people the fundamental importance of the armed fight, and the people themselves who rise in rebellion and teach the leaders these practical necessities of which we speak. Thus, as a product of this interaction between the guerrilla fighter and his people, a progressive radicalization appears which further accentuates the revolutionary characteristics of the movement and gives it a national scope.

2. THE GUERRILLA FIGHTER AS COMBATANT

The life and activities of the guerrilla fighter, sketched thus in their general lines, call for a series of physical, mental, and moral qualities needed for adapting oneself to prevailing conditions and for fulfilling completely any mission assigned.

To the question as to what the guerrilla soldier should be like, the first answer is that he should preferably be an inhabitant of the zone. If this is the case, he will have friends who will help him; if he belongs to the zone itself, he will know it (and this knowledge of the ground is one of the most important factors in guerrilla warfare); and since he will be habituated to local peculiarities he will be able to do better work, not to mention that he will add to all this the enthusiasm that arises from defending his own people and fighting to change a social regime that hurts his own world.

The guerrilla combatant is a night combatant; to say this is to say at the same time that he must have all the special qualities that such fighting requires. He must be cunning and able to march to the place of attack across plains or mountains without anybody's noticing him, and then to fall upon the enemy, taking advantage of the factor of surprise which deserves to be emphasized again as important in this type of fight. After causing panic by this surprise, he should launch himself into the fight implacably without permitting a single weakness in his companions and taking advantage of every sign of weakness on the part of the enemy. Striking like a tornado, destroying all, giving no quarter unless the tactical circumstances call for it, judging those who must be judged, sowing panic among the enemy combatants, he nevertheless treats defenseless prisoners benevolently and shows respect for the dead.

A wounded enemy should be treated with care and respect unless his former life has made him liable to a death penalty, in which case he will be treated in accordance with his deserts. What can never be done is to keep prisoners, unless a secure base of operations, invulnerable to the enemy, has been established. Otherwise, the prisoner will become a dangerous menace to the security of the inhabitants of the region or to the guerrilla band itself because of the information that he can give upon rejoining the enemy army. If he has not been a notorious criminal, he should be set free after receiving a lecture.

The guerrilla combatant ought to risk his life whenever necessary and be ready to die without the least sign of doubt; but, at the same time, he ought to be cautious and never expose himself unnecessarily. All possible precautions ought to be taken to avoid a defeat or an annihilation. For this reason it is extremely important in every fight to maintain vigilance over all the points from which enemy reinforcements may arrive and to take precautions against an encirclement, the consequences of which are usually not physically disastrous but which damages morale by causing a loss of faith in the prospects of the struggle.

However, he ought to be audacious, and, after carefully analyzing the dangers and possibilities in an action, always ready to take an optimistic attitude toward circumstances and to see reasons for a favorable decision even in moments when the analysis of the adverse and favorable conditions does not show an appreciable positive balance.

To be able to survive in the midst of these conditions of life and enemy action, the guerrilla fighter must have a degree of adaptability that will permit him to identify himself with the environment in which he lives, to become a part of it, and to take advantage of it as his ally to the maximum possible extent. He also needs a faculty of rapid comprehension and an instantaneous inventiveness that will permit him to change his tactics according to the dominant course of the action.

These faculties of adaptability and inventiveness in popular armies are what ruin the statistics of the warlords and cause them to waver.

The guerrilla fighter must never for any reason leave a wounded companion at the mercy of the enemy troops, because this would be leaving him to an almost certain death. At whatever cost he must be removed from the zone of combat to a secure place. The greatest exertions and the greatest risks must be taken in this task. The guerrilla soldier must be an extraordinary companion.

At the same time he ought to be close-mouthed. Everything that is said and done before him should be kept strictly in his own mind. He ought never to permit himself a single useless word, even with his own comrades in arms, since the enemy will always try to introduce spies into the ranks of the guerrilla band in order to discover its plans, location, and means of life.

Besides the moral qualities that we have mentioned, the guerrilla fighter should possess a series of very important physical qualities. He must be indefatigable. He must be able to produce another effort at the moment when weariness seems intolerable. Profound conviction, expressed in every line of his face, forces him to take another step, and this not the last one, since it will be followed by another and another and another until he arrives at the place designated by his chiefs.

He ought to be able to endure extremities, to withstand not only the privations of food, water, clothing, and shelter to which he is subjected frequently, but also the sickness and wounds that often must be cured by nature without much help from the surgeon. This is all the more necessary because usually the individual who leaves the guerrilla zone to recover from sickness or wounds will be assassinated by the enemy.

To meet these conditions he needs an iron constitution that will enable him to resist all these adversities without falling ill and to make of his hunted animal's life one more factor of strength. With the help of his natural adaptability, he becomes a part of the land itself where he fights.

All these considerations bring us to ask: what is the ideal age for the guerrilla fighter? These limits are always very difficult to state precisely, because individual and social peculiarities change the figure. A peasant, for example, will be much more resistant than a man from the city. A city dweller who is accustomed to physical exercise and a healthy life will be much more efficient than a man who has lived all his life behind a desk. But generally the maximum age of combatants in the completely nomadic stage of the guerrilla struggle ought not to exceed forty years, although there will be exceptional cases, above all among the peasants. One of the heroes of our struggle, Comandante Crescencio Perez, entered the Sierra at 65 years of age and was immediately one of the most useful men in the troop.

We might also ask if the members of the guerrilla band should be drawn from a certain social class. It has already been said that this social composition ought to be adjusted to that of the zone chosen for the center of operations, which is to say that the combatant nucleus of the guerrilla army ought to be made up of peasants. The peasant is evidently the best soldier; but the other strata of the population are not by any means to be excluded nor deprived of the opportunity to fight for a just cause. Individual exceptions are also very important in this respect.

We have not yet fixed the lower limit of age. We believe that minors less than sixteen years of age ought not to be accepted for the fight, except in very special circumstances. In general these young boys, nearly children, do not have sufficient development to bear up under the work, the weather, and the suffering to which they will be subjected.

The best age for a guerrilla fighter varies between 25 and 35 years, a stage in which the life of most persons has assumed definite shape. Whoever sets out at that age, abandoning his home, his children, and his entire world, must have thought well of his responsibility and reached a firm decision not to retreat a step. There are extraordinary cases of children who as combatants have reached the highest ranks of our rebel army, but this is not the usual case. For every one of them who displayed great fighting qualities, there were tens who ought to have been returned to their homes and who frequently constituted a dangerous burden for the guerrilla band.

The guerrilla fighter, as we have said, is a soldier who carries his house on his back like the snail; therefore, he must arrange his knapsack in such a way that the smallest quantity of utensils will render the greatest possible service. He will carry only the indispensable, but he will take care of it at all times as something fundamental and not to be lost except in extremely adverse situations.

His armament will also be only that which he can carry on his own. Reprovisioning is very difficult, above all with bullets. To keep them dry, always to keep them clean, to count them one by one so that none is lost; these are the watchwords. And the gun ought always to be kept clean, well greased, and with the barrel shining. It is advisable for the chief of each group to impose some penalty or punishment on those who do not maintain their armaments in these conditions.

People with such notable devotion and firmness must have an ideal that sustains them in the adverse conditions that we have described. This ideal is simple, without great pretensions, and in general does not go very far; but it is so firm, so clear that one will give his life for it without the least hesitation. With almost all peasants this ideal is the right to have and work a piece of land of their own and to enjoy just social treatment. Among workers it is to have work, to receive an adequate wage as well as just social treatment. Among students and professional people more abstract ideas such as liberty are found to be motives for the fight.

This brings us to the question: what is the life of the guerrilla fighter like? His normal life is the long hike. Let us take as an example a mountain guerrilla fighter located in wooded regions under constant harassment by the enemy. In these conditions the guerrilla band moves during daylight hours, without eating, in order to change its position; when night arrives, camp is set up in a clearing near a water supply according to a routine, each group assembling in order to eat in common; at dusk the fires are lighted with whatever is at hand.

The guerrilla fighter eats when he can and everything he can. Sometimes fabulous feasts disappear in the gullet of the combatant; at other times he fasts for two or three days without suffering any diminution in his capacity for work.

His house will be the open sky; between it and his

hammock he places a sheet of waterproof nylon and beneath the cloth and hammock he places his knapsack, gun, and ammunition, which are the treasures of the guerrilla fighter. At times it is not wise for shoes to be removed, because of the possibility of a surprise attack by the enmey. Shoes are another of his precious treasures. Whoever has a pair of them has the security of a happy existence within the limits of the prevailing circumstances.

Thus, the guerrilla fighter will live for days without approaching any inhabited place, avoiding all contact that has not been previously arranged, staying in the wildest zones, knowing hunger, at times thirst, cold, heat; sweating during the continuous marches, letting the sweat dry on his body and adding to it new sweat without any possibility of regular cleanliness (although this also depends somewhat upon the individual disposition, as does everything else).

During the recent war, upon entering the village of El Uvero following a march of sixteen kilometers and a fight of two hours and forty-five minutes in a hot sun (all added to several days passed in very adverse conditions along the sea with intense heat from a boiling sun) our bodies gave off a peculiar and offensive odor that repelled anyone who came near. Our noses were completely habituated to this type of life; the hammocks of guerrilla fighters are known for their characteristic, individual odor.

In such conditions breaking camp ought to be done rapidly, leaving no traces behind; vigilance must be extreme. For every ten men sleeping there ought to be one or two on watch, with the sentinels being changed continually and a sharp vigil being maintained over all entrances to the camp.

Campaign life teaches several tricks for preparing meals, some to help speed their preparation; others to add seasoning with little things found in the forest; still others for inventing new dishes that give a more varied character to the guerrilla menu, which is composed mainly of roots, grains, salt, a little oil or lard, and, very sporadically, pieces of the meat of some animal that has been slain. This refers to the life of a group operating in tropical sectors.

Within the framework of the combatant life, the most interesting event, the one that carries all to a convulsion of joy and puts new vigor in everybody's steps, is the battle. The battle, climax of the guerrilla life, is sought at an opportune moment either when an enemy encampment sufficiently weak to be annihilated has been located and investigated; or when an enemy column is advancing directly toward the territory occupied by the liberating force. The two cases are different.

Against an encampment the action will be a thin encirclement and fundamentally will become a hunt for the members of the columns that come to break the encirclement. An entrenched enemy is never the favorite prey of the guerrilla fighter; he prefers his enemy to be on the move, nervous, not knowing the ground, fearful of everything and without natural protections for defense. Whoever is behind a parapet with powerful arms for repelling an offensive will never be in the plight, however bad his situation, of a long column that is attacked suddenly in two or three places and cut. If the attackers are not able to encircle the column and destroy it totally, they will retire prior to any counteraction.

If there is no possibility of defeating those entrenched in a camp by means of hunger or thirst or by a direct assault, the guerrilla ought to retire after the encirclement has yielded its fruits of destruction in the relieving columns. In cases where the guerrilla column is too weak and the invading column too strong, the action should be concentrated upon the vanguard. There should be a special preference for this tactic, whatever the hoped-for result, since after the leading ranks have been struck several times, thus diffusing among the soldiers the news that death is constantly occurring to those in the van, the reluctance to occupy those places will provoke nothing less than mutiny. Therefore, attacks ought to be made on that point even if they are also made at other points of the column.

The facility with which the guerrilla fighter can perform his function and adapt himself to the environment will depend upon his equipment. Even though joined with others in small groups, he has individual characteristics. He should have in his knapsack, besides his regular shelter, everything necessary to survival in case he finds himself alone for some time.

In giving the list of equipment we will refer essentially to that which should be carried by an individual located in rough country at the beginning of a war, with frequent rainfall, some cold weather, and harassment by the enemy; in other words, we place ourselves in the situation that existed at the beginning of the Cuban war of liberation.

The equipment of the guerrilla fighter is divided into the essential and the accessory. Among the first is a hammock. This provides adequate rest; it is easy to find two trees from which it can be strung; and, in cases where one sleeps on the ground, it can serve as a mattress. Whenever it is raining or the ground is wet, a frequent occurrence in tropical mountain zones, the hammock is indispensable for sleeping. A piece of waterproof nylon cloth is its complement. The nylon should be large enough to cover the hammock when tied from its four corners, and with a line strung through the center to the same trees from which the hammock hangs. This last line serves to make the nylon into a kind of tent by raising a center ridge and causing it to shed water.

A blanket is indispensable, because it is cold in the mountains at night. It is also necessary to carry a gar-

HAMMOCK WITH A NYLON ROOF.

ment such as a jacket or coat which will enable one to bear the extreme changes of temperature. Clothing should consist of rough work trousers and shirt, which may or may not be of a uniform cloth. Shoes should be of the best possible construction and also, since without good shoes marches are very difficult, they should be one of the first articles laid up in reserve.

Since the guerrilla fighter carries his house in his knapsack, the latter is very important. The more primitive types may be made from any kind of sack carried by two ropes; but those of canvas found in the market or made by a harness maker are preferable. The guerrilla fighter ought always to carry some personal food besides that which the troop carries or consumes in its camps. Indispensable articles are: lard or oil, which is necessary for fat consumption; canned goods, which should not be consumed except in circumstances where food for cooking cannot be found or when there are too many cans and their weight impedes the march; preserved fish, which has great nutritional value; condensed milk, which is also nourishing, particularly on account of the large quantity of sugar that it contains; some sweet for its good taste. Powdered milk can also be carried. Sugar is another essential part of the supplies, as is salt, without which life becomes sheer martyrdom, and something that serves to season the meals, such as onion, garlic, etc., according to the characteristics of the country. This completes the category of the essentials.

The guerrilla fighter should carry a plate, knife, and fork, camping style, which will serve all the various necessary functions. The plate can be camping or military type or a pan that is usable for cooking anything from a piece of meat to a "malanga" or a potato, or for brewing tea or coffee.

To care for the rifle, special greases are necessary; and these must be carefully administered—sewing machine oil is very good if there is no special oil available. Also needed are cloths that will serve for cleaning the arms frequently and a rod for cleaning the gun inside, something that ought to be done often. The ammunition belt can be of commercial type or homemade, according to the circumstances, but it ought to be so made that not a single bullet will be lost. Ammunition is the basis of the fight without which everything else would be in vain; it must be cared for like gold.

A canteen or a bottle for water is essential, since it will frequently be necessary to drink in a situation where water is not available. Among medicines, those of general use should be carried: for example, penicillin or some other type of antibiotic, preferably the types taken orally, carefully closed; medicines for lowering fever, such as aspirin; and others adapted to treating the endemic diseases of the area. These may be tablets against malaria, sulfas for diarrhea, medicines against parasites of all types; in other words, fit the medicine to the characteristics of the region. It is advisable in places where there are poisonous animals to carry appropriate injections. Surgical instruments will complete the medical equipment. Small personal items for taking care of less important injuries should also be included.

A customary and extremely important comfort in the life of the guerrilla fighter is a smoke, whether cigars, cigarettes, or pipe tobacco; a smoke in moments of rest is a great friend to the solitary soldier. Pipes are useful, because they permit using to the extreme all tobacco that remains in the butts of cigars and cigarettes at time of scarcity. Matches are extremely important, not only for lighting a smoke, but also for starting fires; this is one of the great problems in the forest in rainy periods. It is preferable to carry both matches and a lighter, so that if the lighter runs out of fuel, matches remain as a substitute.

Soap should be carried, not only for personal cleanliness, but for washing eating utensils, because intestinal infections or irritations are frequent and can be caused by spoiled food left on dirty cooking ware. With this set of equipment, the guerrilla fighter can be assured that he will be able to live in the forest under adverse conditions, no matter how bad, for as long as is necessary to dominate the situation.

There are accessories that at times are useful and others that constitute a bother but are very useful. The compass is one of these; at the outset this will be used a great deal in gaining orientation, but little by little knowledge of the country will make it unnecessary. In mountainous regions a compass is not of much use, since the route it indicates will usually be cut off by impassable obstacles. Another useful article is an extra nylon cloth for covering all equipment when it rains. Remember that rain in tropical countries is continuous during certain months and that water is the enemy of all the things that the guerrilla fighter must carry: food, ammunition, medicine, paper, and clothing.

A change of clothing can be carried, but this is usually a mark of inexperience. The usual custom is to carry no more than an extra pair of pants, eliminating extra underwear and other articles, such as towels. The life of the guerrilla fighter teaches him to conserve his energy in carrying his knapsack from one place to another, and he will, little by little, get rid of everything that does not have essential value.

In addition to a piece of soap, useful for washing utensils as well as for personal cleanliness, a toothbrush and paste should be carried. It is worthwhile also to carry a book, which will be exchanged with other members of the band. These books can be good biographies of past heroes, histories, or economic geographies, preferably of the country, and works of general character that will serve to raise the cultural level of the soldiers and discourage the tendency toward gambling or other undesirable forms of passing the time. There are periods of boredom in the life of the guerrilla fighter.

Whenever there is extra space in the knapsack, it ought to be used for food, except in those zones where the food supply is easy and sure. Sweets or food of lesser importance complementing the basic items can be carried. Crackers can be one of these, although they occupy a large space and break up into crumbs. In thick forests a machete is useful; in very wet places a small bottle of gasoline or light resinous wood, such as pine, for kindling will make firebuilding easier when the wood is wet.

A small notebook and pen or pencil for taking notes and for letters to the outside or communication with other guerrilla bands ought always to be a part of the guerrilla fighter's equipment. Pieces of string or rope should be kept available; these have many uses. Also needles, thread, and buttons for clothing. The guerrilla fighter who carries this equipment will have a solid house on his back, rather heavy but furnished to assure a comfortable life during the hardships of the campaign.

3. ORGANIZATION OF A GUERRILLA BAND

No rigid scheme can be offered for the organization of a guerrilla band; there will be innumerable differences according to the environment in which it is to operate. For convenience of exposition we will suppose that our experience has a universal application, but it should be kept in mind always that there will possibly be new forms that comport better with the particular characteristics of a given armed group.

The size of the component units of the guerrilla force is one of the most difficult problems to deal with: there will be different numbers of men and different compositions of the troop, as we have already explained. Let us suppose a force situated in favorable ground, mountainous, with conditions not so bad as to necessitate perpetual flight, but not so good as to afford a base of operations. The combat units of an armed force thus situated ought to number not more than one hundred and fifty men, and even this number is rather high; ideal would be a unit of about one hundred men. This constitutes a column, and in the Cuban organization is commanded by a comandante. It should be remembered that in our war the grades of corporal and sergeant were omitted because they were considered reminiscent of the tyranny.[4]

On this premise, the comandante commands this whole force of one hundred to one hundred fifty men; and there will be as many captains as there are groups of thirty to forty men. The captain has the function of directing and unifying his platoon, making it fight almost always as a unit and looking after the distribution of men and the general organization. In guerrilla warfare, the squad is the functional unit. Each squad, made up of approximately eight to twelve men, is commanded by a lieutenant, who performs for his group functions analogous to those of the captain, to whom he must always be in constant subordination.

The operational tendency of the guerrilla band to function in small groups makes the squad the true unit. Eight to ten men are the maximum that can act as a unit in a fight in these conditions: therefore, the squad, which will frequently be separated from the captain even though they fight on the same front, will operate under the orders of its lieutenant; there are exceptions, of course. A squad should not be broken up nor kept dispersed at times when there is no fighting. Each squad and platoon should know who the immediate successor is in case the chief falls, and these persons should be sufficiently trained to be able to take over their new responsibilities immediately.

One of the fundamental problems of the troop is food supply; in this everyone from the last man to the chief must be treated alike. This acquires a high importance, not only because of the chronic shortage of supplies, but also because meals are the only events that take place daily. The troops, who have a keen sense of justice, measure the rations with a sharp eye; the least favoritism for anyone ought never to be

[4] Fulgencio Batista first came to power in Cuba as a result of a "sergeants' revolt" against Gerardo Machado in 1933.

permitted. If in certain circumstances the meal is served to the whole column, a regular order should be established and observed strictly, and at the same time the quantity and quality of food given to each one ought to be carefully checked. In the distribution of clothing the problem is different, these being articles of individual use. Here two considerations prevail: first, the demand for necessities of those who need them, which will almost always be greater than the supply; and, second, the length of service and merits of each one of the applicants. The length of service and merits, something very difficult to fix exactly, should be noted in special booklets by one assigned this responsibility under the direct supervision of the chief of the column. The same should be said about other articles that become available and are of individual rather than collective utility. Tobacco and cigarettes ought to be distributed according to the general rule of equal treatment for everybody.

This task of distribution should be a specifically assigned responsibility. It is preferable that the persons designated be attached directly to the command. The command performs, therefore, administrative tasks of liaison which are very important, as well as all the other special tasks that are necessary. Officers of the greatest intelligence ought to be in it. Soldiers attached to the command ought to be alert and of maximum dedication, since their burdens will usually be greater than those borne by the rest of the troop. Nevertheless, they can have no special treatment at mealtime.

Each guerrilla fighter carries his complete equipment; there is also a series of implements of use to the group that should be equitably distributed within the column. For this, too, rules can be established, depending upon the number of unarmed persons in the troop. One system is to distribute all extra materiel, such as medicines, medical or dental or surgical instruments, extra food, clothing, general supplies, and heavy weapons equally among all platoons, which will then be responsible for their custody. Each captain will distribute these supplies among the squads, and each chief of squad will distribute them among his men. Another solution, which can be used when a part of the troop is not armed, is to create special squads or platoons assigned to transport; this works out well, since it leaves the soldier who already has the weight and responsibility of his rifle free of extra cargo. In this way danger of losing materiel is reduced, since it is concentrated; and at the same time there is an incentive for the porter to carry more and to carry better and to demonstrate more enthusiasm, since in this way he will win his right to a weapon in the future. These platoons will march in the rear positions and will have the same duties and the same treatment as the rest of the troop.

The tasks to be carried out by a column will vary according to its activities. If it is encamped, there will be special teams for keeping watch. These should be experienced, specially trained, and they should receive some special reward for this duty. This can consist of increased independence, or, if there is an excess of sweets or tobacco after proportional distribution to each column, something extra for the members of those units that carry out special tasks. For example, if there are one hundred men and one hundred and fifteen packages of cigarettes, the fifteen extra packs of cigarettes can be distributed among the members of the units referred to. The vanguard and the rearguard units, separated from the rest, will have special duties of vigilance; but, besides, each platoon ought to have such a watch of its own. The farther from the encampment the watch is maintained, the greater is the security of the group, especially when it is in open country.

The places chosen should be high, dominating a

wide area by day and difficult to approach by night. If the plan is to stay several days, it is worthwhile to construct defenses that will permit a sustained fire in case of an attack. These defenses can be obliterated when the guerrilla band moves, or they can be left if circumstances no longer make it necessary to hide the path of the column.

In places where permanent encampments are established, the defenses ought to be improved constantly. Remember that in a mountainous zone on ground carefully chosen, the only heavy arm that is effective is the mortar. Using roofs reinforced with materials from the region, such as wood, rocks, etc., it is possible to make good refuges which are difficult for the enemy forces to approach and which will afford protection from mortar shells for the guerrilla forces.

It is very important to maintain discipline in the camp, and this should have an educational function. The guerrilla fighters should be required to go to bed and get up at fixed hours. Games that have no social function and that hurt the morale of the troops and the consumption of alcoholic drinks should both be prohibited. All these tasks are performed by a commission of internal order elected from those combatants of greatest revolutionary merit. Another mission of these persons is to prevent the lighting of fires in places visible from a distance or that raise columns of smoke before nightfall; also to see that the camp is kept clean and that it is left in such a condition when the column leaves as to show no signs of passage, if this is necessary.

Great care must be taken with fires which leave traces for a long time. They must be covered with earth; papers, cans, and scraps of food should also be burned. During the march complete silence must prevail in the column. Orders are passed by gestures or by whispers that go from mouth to mouth until they reach the last man. If the guerrilla band is marching through unknown places, breaking a road, or being led by a guide, the vanguard will be approximately one hundred or two hundred meters or even more in front, according to the characteristics of the ground. In places where confusion may arise as to the route, a man will be left at each turning to await those who follow, and this will be repeated until the last man in the rearguard has passed. The rearguard will also be somewhat separated from the rest of the column, keeping a watch on the roads in the rear and trying to erase tracks of the troops as much as possible. If there is a road coming from the side that offers danger, it is necessary always to have a group keeping a watch on it until the last man has passed. It is more practical that each platoon utilize its own men for this special duty, with each having the obligation to pass the guard to members of the following platoon and then to rejoin his own unit; this process will be continued until the whole troop has passed.

The march should be uniform and in an established order, always the same. Thus it will always be known that Platoon #1 is the vanguard, followed by Platoon #2 and then Platoon #3, which may be the command; then #4, followed by the rearguard or Platoon #5 or other platoons that make up the column, always in the same order. In night marches silence should be even stricter and the distance between each combatant shorter, so that no one will get lost and make it necessary to shout and turn on lights. Light is the enemy of the guerrilla fighter at nighttime.

If all this marching has attack as its objective, then upon arriving at a given point, the point to which all will return after the objective has been accomplished, extra weight will be set down, such things as knapsacks and cooking utensils, for example, and each platoon will proceed with nothing more than its arms and fighting equipment. The point of attack should have been already studied by trustworthy people who have reconnoitered the ground and have observed the location of the enemy guards. The leaders, knowing the orientation of the base, the number of men that defend it, etc., will make the final plan for the attack and send combatants to their places, always keeping in mind that a good part of the troops should be assigned to intercept reinforcements. In cases where the attack upon the base is to be merely a diversion in order to provoke the sending of reinforcements along roads that can be easily ambushed, a man should communicate the result rapidly to the command as soon as the attack has been carried out, in order to break the encirclement, if necessary to prevent being attacked from the rear. In any case there must always be a watch on the roads that lead to the place of combat while the encirclement or direct attack is being carried out.

By night a direct attack is always preferable. It is possible to capture an encampment if there is enough drive and necessary presence of mind and if the risks are not excessive.

An encirclement requires waiting and taking cover, closing in steadily on the enemy, trying to harass him in every way, and, above all, trying to force him by fire to come out. When the circle has been closed to short range, the "Molotov cocktail" is a weapon of extraordinary effectiveness.[5] Before arriving at a range for the "cocktail," shotguns with a special charge can be employed. These arms, christened in our war with the name of "M-16," consist of a 16-calibre sawed-off shotgun with a pair of legs added in such a way that with the butt of the gun they form a tripod. The weapon will thus be mounted at an angle of about 45 degrees; this can be varied by moving the legs back and forth. It is loaded with an open shell from which

[5] A Molotov cocktail is a bottle containing three parts kerosene and one part motor oil. The bottle is sealed and wrapped in waste cotton, which is sprinkled with gasoline and ignited. When hurled against a target the bottle breaks and burning kerosene spreads a sheet of flame.

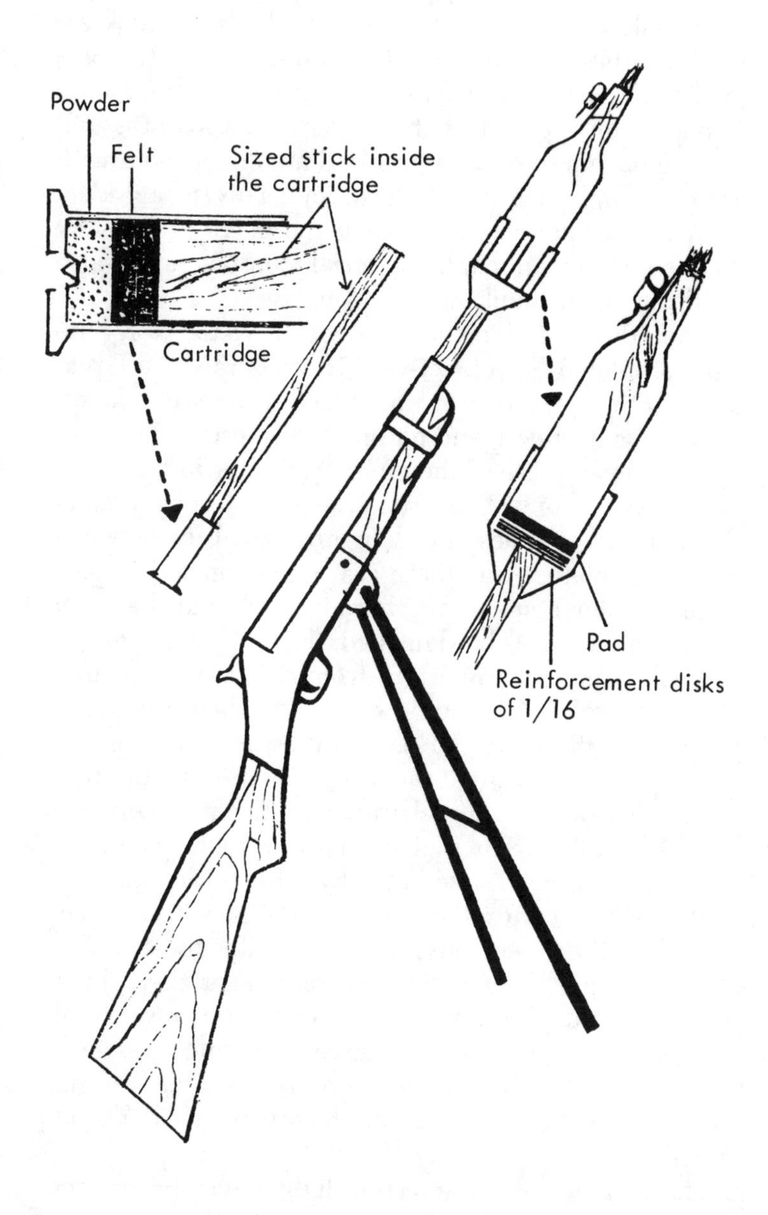

ADAPTATION OF THE "MOLOTOV COCKTAIL" TO A RIFLE.

all the shot has been removed. A cylindrical stick extending from the muzzle of the gun is used as the projectile. A bottle of gasoline resting on a rubber base is placed on the end of the stick. This apparatus will fire the burning bottles a hundred meters or more with a fairly high degree of accuracy. This is an ideal weapon for encirclements when the enemy has many wooden or inflammable material constructions; also for firing against tanks in hilly country.

Once the encirclement ends with a victory, or, having completed its objectives, is withdrawn, all platoons retire in order to the place where the knapsacks have been left, and normal life is resumed.

The nomadic life of the guerrilla fighter in this stage produces not only a deep sense of fraternity among the men but at times also dangerous rivalries between groups or platoons. If these are not channeled to produce beneficial emulation, there is a risk that the unity of the column will be damaged. The education of the guerrilla fighter is important from the very beginning of the struggle. This should explain to them the social purpose of the fight and their duties, clarify their understanding, and give them lessons in morale that serve to forge their characters. Each experience should be a new source of strength for victory and not simply one more episode in the fight for survival.

One of the great educational techniques is example. Therefore the chiefs must constantly offer the example of a pure and devoted life. Promotion of the soldier should be based on valor, capacity, and a spirit of sacrifice; whoever does not have these qualities in a high degree ought not to have responsible assignments, since he will cause unfortunate accidents at any moment.

The conduct of the guerrilla fighter will be subject to judgment whenever he approaches a house to ask for something. The inhabitants will draw favorable or unfavorable conclusions about the guerrilla band according to the manner in which any service or food or other necessity is solicited and the methods used to get what is wanted. The explanation by the chief should be detailed about these problems, emphasizing their importance; he should also teach by example. If a town is entered, all drinking of alcohol should be prohibited and the troops should be exhorted beforehand to give the best possible example of discipline. The entrances and exits to the town should be constantly watched.

The organization, combat capacity, heroism, and spirit of the guerrilla band will undergo a test of fire during an encirclement by the enemy, which is the most dangerous situation of the war. In the jargon of our guerrilla fighters in the recent war, the phrase "encirclement face" was given to the face of fear worn by someone who was frightened. The hierarchy of the deposed regime pompously spoke of its campaigns of "encirclement and annihilation." However, for a guerrilla band that knows the country and that is united ideologically and emotionally with its chief, this is not a particularly serious problem. It need only take cover, try to slow up the advance of the enemy, impede his action with heavy equipment, and await nightfall, the natural ally of the guerrilla fighter. Then with the greatest possible stealth, after exploring and choosing the best road, the band will depart, utilizing the most adequate means of escape and maintaining absolute silence. It is extremely difficult in these conditions at night to prevent a group of men from escaping the encirclement.

4. THE COMBAT

Combat is the most important drama in the guerrilla life. It occupies only a short time; nevertheless, these brilliant moments acquire an extraordinary importance, since each small encounter is a battle of a fundamental kind for the combatants.

We have already pointed out that an attack should be carried out in such a way as to give a guarantee of victory. In addition to general observations concerning the tactical function of attack in guerrilla warfare, the different characteristics that each action can present ought to be noted. We will refer initially, for purposes of description, to the type of fight carried out on favorable ground, because this is the original model of guerrilla warfare; and it is in this connection that certain principles must be examined before dealing with other problems through a study of practical experience. Warfare on the plain is always the result of an advance by the guerrilla bands consequent on their being strengthened and on changes in conditions; this implies an increase of experience on the part of the guerrilla and with it the possibility of using that experience to advantage.

In the first stage of guerrilla warfare, enemy columns will penetrate insurgent territory deeply; depending on the strength of these columns two different types of guerrilla attacks will be made. One of these, first in chronological order, is for a fixed number of months to cause systematic losses in the enemy's offensive capacity. This tactic is carried out on the vanguards. Unfavorable ground impedes flank defenses by the advancing columns; therefore, there must always be one point of the vanguard that, as it penetrates and exposes the lives of its components, serves to give security to the rest of the column. When men and reserves are insufficient and the enemy is strong, the guerrilla should always aim for the destruction of this vanguard point. The system is simple; only a certain coordination is necessary. At the moment when the vanguard appears at the selected place—the steepest possible—a deadly fire is let loose on them, after a convenient number of men have been allowed to penetrate. A small group must hold the rest of the column for some moments while arms, munitions, and equipment are being collected. The guerrilla soldier ought always to have in mind that his source of supply of arms is the enemy and that, except in special circumstances, he ought not to engage in a battle that will not lead to the capture of such equipment.

When the strength of the guerrilla band permits, a complete encirclement of the column will be carried out; or at least this impression will be given. In this case the guerrilla front line must be strong enough and well enough covered to resist the frontal assaults of the enemy, considering, naturally, both offensive power and combat morale. At the moment in which the enemy is detained in some chosen place, the rear-guard guerrilla forces make an attack on the enemy's rear. Such a chosen place will have characteristics making a flank maneuver difficult; snipers, outnumbered, perhaps, by eight or ten times, will have the whole enemy column within the circle of fire. Whenever there are sufficient forces in these cases, all roads should be protected with ambushes in order to detain reinforcements. The encirclement will be closed gradually, above all at night. The guerrilla fighter knows the places where he fights, the invading column does not; the guerrilla fighter grows at night, and the enemy feels his fear growing in the darkness.

In this way, without too much difficulty, a column can be totally destroyed; or at least such losses can be inflicted upon it as to prevent its returning to battle and to force it to take a long time for regrouping.

When the force of the guerrilla band is small and it is desired above all to detain and slow down the advance of the invading column, groups of snipers fluctuating between two and ten should be distributed all around the column at each of the four cardinal points. In this situation combat can be begun, for example, on the right flank; when the enemy centers his action on that flank and fires on it, shooting will begin at that moment from the left flank; at another moment from the rearguard or from the vanguard; and so forth.

With a very small expenditure of ammunition it is possible to hold the enemy in check indefinitely.

The technique of attacking an enemy convoy or position must be adapted to the conditions of the place chosen for the combat. In general, the first attack on an encircled place should be made during night hours against an advance post, with surprise assured. A surprise attack carried out by skillful commandos can easily liquidate a position, thanks to the advantage of surprise. For a regular encirclement the paths of escape can be controlled with a few men and the roads of access defended with ambushes; these should be distributed in such a way that if one is unsuccessful, it falls back or simply withdraws, while a second remains, and so on successively. In cases where the surprise factor is not present, victory in an attempt to take an encampment will depend on the capacity of the encircling force to detain the attempts of the rescue columns. In these cases there will usually be support on the enemy's side by artillery, mortars, airplanes, and tanks. In favorable ground the tank is an arm of small danger; it must travel by roads that are narrow and is an easy victim of mines. The offensive capacity of these vehicles when in formation is here generally absent or reduced, since they must proceed in Indian file or at most two abreast. The best and surest weapon against the tank is the mine; but in a close fight, which may easily take place in steep places, the "Molotov cocktail" is an arm of extraordinary value. We will not talk yet of the bazooka, which for the guerrilla force is a decisive weapon but difficult to acquire, at least in the first stages. Against the mortar there is the recourse of a trench with a roof. The mortar is an arm of formidable potency when used against an encircled place; but on the other hand, against mobile attackers it loses its effectiveness unless it is used in large batteries. Artillery does not have great importance in this type of fight, since it has to be placed in locations of convenient access and it does not see the targets, which are constantly shifting. Aviation constitutes the principal arm of the oppressor forces, but its power of attack also is much reduced by the fact that its only targets are small trenches, generally hidden. Planes will be able to drop high-explosive or napalm bombs, both of which constitute inconveniences rather than true dangers. Besides, as the guerrilla draws as close as possible to the defensive lines of the enemy, it becomes very difficult for planes to attack these points of the vanguard effectively.

When encampments with wood or inflammable constructions are attacked, the "Molotov cocktail" is a very important arm at a short distance. At longer distances bottles with inflammable material with the fuse lighted can be launched from a sixteen-calibre shotgun, as described earlier.

Of all the possible types of mines, the most effective, although requiring the most technical capacity, is the remotely exploded mine; but contact, fuse, and above all electric mines with their lengths of cord are also extremely useful and constitute on mountainous roads defenses for the popular forces that are virtually invulnerable.

A good defense against armored cars along roads is to dig sloping ditches in such a way that the tank enters them easily and afterwards cannot get out, as the picture shows. These can easily be hidden from the enemy, especially at nighttime or when he has no infantry in advance of the tanks because of resistance by the guerrilla forces.

Another common form of advance by the enemy in

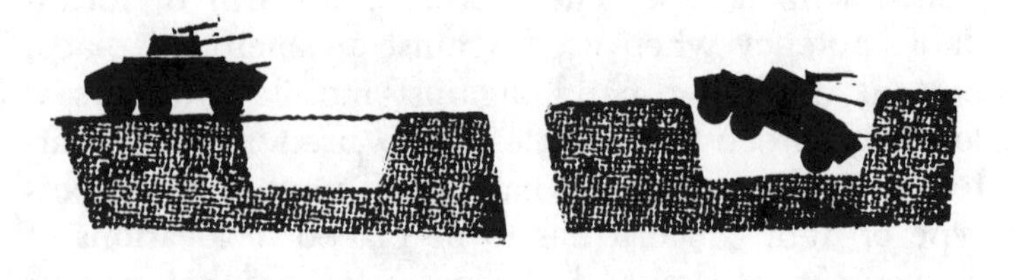

ANTI-TANK TRAP.

zones that are not too steep is in trucks that are more or less open. The columns are headed by armored vehicles and the infantry follows behind in trucks. Depending upon the force of the guerrilla band it may be possible to encircle the entire column, following the general rules; or it can be split by attacking some of the trucks and simultaneously exploding mines. It is necessary to act rapidly in this case, seizing the arms of the fallen enemy and retiring.

For an attack on open trucks, an arm of great importance which should be used with all its potential is the shotgun. A sixteen-calibre shotgun with large shot can sweep ten meters, nearly the whole area of the truck, killing some of the occupants, wounding others, and provoking an enormous confusion. Grenades, if they are available, are also excellent weapons for these cases.

For all these attacks surprise is fundamental because, at least at the moment of firing the first shot, it is one of the basic requirements of guerrilla warfare. Surprise is not possible if the peasants of the zone know of the presence of the insurgent army. For this reason all movements of attack should be made at night. Only men of proven discretion and loyalty can know of these movements and establish the contacts. The march should be made with knapsacks full of food, in order to be able to live two, three, or four days in the places of ambush.

The discretion of the peasants should never be trusted too much, first because there is a natural tendency to talk and to comment on events with other members of the family or with friends; and also because of the inevitable cruelty with which the enemy soldiers treat the population after a defeat. Terror can be sown, and this terror leads to someone's talking too much, revealing important information, in the effort to save his life.

In general, the place chosen for an ambush should be located at least one day's march from the habitual camp of the guerrilla band, since the enemy will almost always know its location more or less accurately.

We said before that the form of fire in a battle indicates the location of the opposing forces; on one side violent and rapid firing by the soldier of the line, who has the customary abundance of ammunition; on the other side the methodical, sporadic fire of the guerrilla fighter who knows the value of every bullet and who endeavors to expend it with a high degree of economy, never firing one shot more than necessary. It is not reasonable to allow an enemy to escape or to fail to use an ambush to the full in order to save ammunition, but the amount that is to be expended in determined circumstances should be calculated in advance and the action carried out according to these calculations.

Ammunition is the great problem of the guerrilla fighter. Arms can always be obtained. Furthermore, those which are obtained are not expended in guerrilla warfare, while ammunition is expended; also, generally, it is arms with their ammunition that are captured and never or rarely ammunition only. Each weapon that is taken will have its loads, but it cannot contribute to the others because there are no extras. The tactical principle of saving fire is fundamental in this type of warfare.

A guerrilla chief who takes pride in his role will never be careless about withdrawal. This should be timely, rapid, and carried out so as to save all the wounded and the equipment of the guerrilla, its knapsacks, ammunition, etc. The rebels ought never to be surprised while withdrawing, nor can they permit themselves the negligence of becoming surrounded. Therefore, guards must be posted along the chosen road at all places where the enemy army will eventually bring its troops forward in an attempt to close a circle; and there must be a system of communication that will permit rapid reports when a force tries to surround the rebels.

In the combat there must always be some unarmed men. They will recover the guns of companions who are wounded or dead, guns seized in battle or belonging to prisoners; they will take charge of the prisoners, of removing the wounded, and of transmission of messages. Besides, there ought to be a good corps of messengers with iron legs and a proven sense of responsibility who will give the necessary reports in the least possible time.

The number of men needed besides the armed combatants varies; but a general rule is two or three for each ten, including those who will be present at the scene of the battle and those who will carry out necessary tasks in the rearguard, keeping watch on the route of withdrawal and performing the messenger services mentioned above.

When a defensive type of war is being fought, that is to say, when the guerrilla band is endeavoring to prohibit the passage of an invasion column beyond a certain point, the action becomes a war of positions; but always at the outset it should have the factor of surprise. In this case, since trenches as well as other defensive systems that will be easily observable by the peasants are going to be used, it is necessary that these latter remain in the friendly zone. In this type of warfare the government generally establishes a blockade of the region, and the peasants who have not fled must go to buy their basic foods at establishments located outside the zones of guerrilla action. Should these persons leave the region at critical moments, such as those we are now describing, this would constitute a serious danger on account of the information that they could eventually supply to the enemy army. The policy of complete isolation must serve as the strategic principle of the guerrilla army in these cases.

The defenses and the whole defensive apparatus should be arranged in such a manner that the enemy vanguard will always fall into an ambush. It is very important as a psychological factor that the man in the vanguard will die without escape in every battle, because this produces within the enemy army a growing consciousness of this danger, until the moment arrives when nobody wants to be in the vanguard; and it is obvious that a column with no vanguard cannot move, since somebody has to assume that responsibility. Also encirclements can be carried out if these are expedient; or diversionary maneuvers such as flank attacks; or the enemy can simply be detained frontally. In every case, places which are susceptible of being utilized by the enemy for flank attacks should be fortified.

We are now assuming that more men and arms are available than in the combats described hitherto. It is evident that the blockade of all possible roads converging into a zone, which may be very numerous, requires a large personnel. The various kinds of traps and attacks against armored vehicles will be increased here, in order to give the greatest security possible to the systems of fixed trenches which can be located by the enemy. In general in this type of fight the order is to defend the positions unto death if necessary; and it is essential to assure the maximum possibilities of survival to every defender.

The more a trench is hidden from distant view, the better; above all, it is important to give it a cover so that mortar fire will be ineffective. Mortars of 60.1 or 85 millimeters, the usual campaign calibres, cannot penetrate a good roof made with simple materials from the region. This may be made from a base of wood, earth, and rocks covered with some camouflage material. An exit for escape in an extremity must always be constructed, so that the defender may get away with less danger.

The sketch below shows the form in which these defenses were constructed in the Sierra Maestra. They were sufficient to protect us from mortar fire.

This outline clearly indicates that fixed lines of fire do not exist. The lines of fire are something more or less theoretical; they are established at certain critical moments, but they are extremely elastic and permeable on both sides.

What does exist is a wide no man's land. But the

REFUGE AGAINST MORTAR FIRE.

characteristics of no man's land in guerrilla warfare are that it is inhabited by a civil population, and that this civil population collaborates in a certain measure with either of the two sides, even though in an overwhelming majority with the insurrectionary band. These people cannot be removed *en masse* from the zone on account of their numbers and because this would create problems of supply for either one of the contenders who tried to provide food for so many people. This no man's land is penetrated by periodic incursions (generally during the daytime) by the repressive forces and at night by the guerrilla forces. The guerrilla forces find there a maintenance base of great importance for their troops; this should be cared for in a political way, always establishing the best possible relations with the peasants and merchants.

In this type of warfare the tasks of those who do not carry arms, of those who are not direct combatants, are extremely important. We have already indicated some of the characteristics of liaison in places of combat; but liaison is an institution throughout the whole guerrilla organization. Liaison out to the most distant command or out to the most distant group of guerrilla fighters ought to be linked in such a way that messages will travel from one place to another via the most rapid system available in the region. This holds for regions of easy defense, that is to say, in favorable ground, as well as in unfavorable ground. A guerrilla band operating in unfavorable ground will not be able to use modern systems of communication, such as telegraph, roads, etc., except some radios located in military garrisons capable of being defended. If these fall into the hands of the enemy force, it is necessary to change codes and frequencies, a task that is rather troublesome.

In all these matters we are speaking from memory of things that occurred in our war of liberation. The daily and accurate report on all activities of the enemy is complemented with liaison. The system of espionage should be carefully studied, well worked out, and personnel chosen with maximum care. The harm that a counter-spy can do is enormous, but even without such an extreme case, the harm that can result from exaggerated information which misjudges the danger is very great. It is not probable that danger will be underrated. The tendency of people in the country is to overrate and exaggerate it. The same magic mentality that makes phantasms and various supernatural beings appear also creates monstrous armies where there is hardly a platoon or an enemy patrol. The spy ought to seem as neutral as possible, not known by the enemy to have any connection with the forces of liberation. This is not as difficult a task as it appears; many such persons are found in the course of the war: businessmen, professional men, and even clergymen can lend their help in this type of task and give timely information.

One of the most important characteristics of guerrilla warfare is the notable difference between the information that reaches the rebel forces and the information possessed by the enemy. While the latter must operate in regions that are absolutely hostile, finding sullen silence on the part of the peasants, the rebels have in nearly every house a friend or even a relative; and news is passed about constantly through the liaison system until it reaches the central command of the guerrilla force or of the guerrilla group that is in the zone.

When an enemy penetration occurs in territory that has become openly pro-guerrilla, where all the peasants respond to the cause of the people, a serious problem is created. The majority of peasants try to escape with the popular army, abandoning their children and their work; others even carry the whole family; some wait upon events. The most serious problem that an enemy penetration into guerrilla territory can provoke is that of a group of families finding themselves in a tight, at times desperate situation. Maximum help should be given to them, but they must be warned of the troubles that can follow upon a flight into inhospitable zones so far from their habitual places of livelihood, exposed to the hardships that usually befall in such cases.

It is not possible to describe any pattern of repression on the part of the enemies of the people. Although the general methods of repression are always the same, the enemies of the people act in a more or less intensely criminal fashion according to the specific social, historic, and economic circumstances of each place. There are places where the flight of a man into the guerrilla zone, leaving his family and his house, does not provoke any great reaction. There are others where this is enough to provoke the burning or seizure of his belongings, and still others where the flight will bring death to all members of his family. Adequate distribution and organization of the peasants who are going to be affected by an enemy advance must of course be arranged according to the habits that prevail in the war zone or country concerned.

Obviously preparations must be made to expel the enemy from such territory by moving against his supplies, completely cutting his lines of communication, destroying by means of small guerrilla bands his attempts to supply himself, and in general forcing him to devote large quantities of men to his supply problem.

In all these combat situations a very important factor is the correct utilization of reserves wherever battle begins. The guerrilla army, because of its characteristics, can rarely count on reserves, since it always strikes in such a way that the efforts of every individual are regulated and employed at something. Nevertheless, despite these characteristics it should have at some place men ready to respond to an unforeseen development, to detain a counter-offensive, or to take care of a situation at any moment. Within the organization of the guerrilla band, assuming that the conditions and possibilities of the moment permit, a utility platoon can be held in readiness, a platoon that should always go to the places of greatest danger. It can be christened the "suicide platoon" or something similar; this title in reality indicates its functions. This "suicide platoon" should be in every place where a battle is decided: in the surprise attacks upon the vanguard, in the defense of the most vulnerable and dangerous places, in a word, wherever the enemy threatens to break the stability of the line of fire. It ought to be made up strictly of volunteers. Entrance into this platoon should be regarded almost as a prize for merit. In time it becomes the favorite group of any guerrilla column, and the guerrilla fighter who wears its insignia enjoys the admiration and respect of all his companions.

5. BEGINNING, DEVELOPMENT, AND END OF A GUERRILLA WAR

We have now abundantly defined the nature of guerrilla warfare. Let us next describe the ideal development of such a war from its beginning as a rising by a single nucleus on favorable ground.

In other words, we are going to theorize once more on the basis of the Cuban experience. At the outset there is a more or less homogeneous group, with some arms, that devotes itself almost exclusively to hiding in the wildest and most inaccessible places, making little contact with the peasants. It strikes a fortunate blow and its fame grows. A few peasants, dispossessed of their land or engaged in a struggle to conserve it, and young idealists of other classes join the nucleus; it acquires greater audacity and starts to operate in inhabited places, making more contact with the people of the zone; it repeats attacks, always fleeing after making them; suddenly it engages in combat with some column or other and destroys its vanguard. Men continue to join it; it has increased in number, but its organization remains exactly the same; its caution diminishes, and it ventures into more populous zones.

Later it sets up temporary camps for several days; it abandons these upon receiving news of the approach of the enemy army, or upon suffering bombardments, or simply upon becoming suspicious that such risks have arisen. The numbers in the guerrilla band increase as work among the masses operates to make of each peasant an enthusiast for the war of liberation. Finally, an inaccessible place is chosen, a settled life is initiated, and the first small industries begin to be established: a shoe factory, a cigar and cigarette factory, a clothing factory, an arms factory, a bakery, hospitals, possibly a radio transmitter, a printing press, etc.

The guerrilla band now has an organization, a new structure. It is the head of a large movement with all the characteristics of a small government. A court is established for the administration of justice, possibly laws are promulgated and the work of indoctrination of the peasant masses continues, extended also to workers if there are any near, to draw them to the cause. An enemy action is launched and defeated; the number of rifles increases; with these the number of men fighting with the guerrilla band increases. A moment arrives when its radius of action will not have increased in the same proportion as its personnel; at that moment a force of appropriate size is separated, a column or a platoon, perhaps, and this goes to another place of combat.

The work of this second group will begin with somewhat different characteristics because of the experience that it brings and because of the influence of the troops of liberation on the war zone. The original nucleus also continues to grow; it has now received substantial support in food, sometimes in guns, from various places; men continue to arrive; the administration of government, with the promulgation of laws, continues; schools are established, permitting the indoctrination and training of recruits. The leaders learn steadily as the war develops, and their capacity of command grows under the added responsibilities of the qualitative and quantitative increases in their forces.

If there are distant territories, a group departs for them at a certain moment, in order to confirm the advances that have been made and to continue the cycle.

But there will also exist an enemy territory, unfavorable for guerrilla warfare. There small groups begin to penetrate, assaulting the roads, destroying bridges, planting mines, sowing disquiet. With the ups and downs characteristic of warfare the movement continues to grow; by this time the extensive work among the masses makes easy movement of the forces possible in unfavorable territory and so opens the final stage, which is suburban guerrilla warfare.

Sabotage increases considerably in the whole zone. Life is paralyzed; the zone is conquered. The guerrillas then go into other zones, where they fight with the enemy army along defined fronts; by now heavy arms have been captured, perhaps even some tanks; the fight is more equal. The enemy falls when the process of partial victories becomes transformed into final victories, that is to say, when the enemy is brought to accept battle in conditions imposed by the guerrilla band; there he is annihilated and his surrender compelled.

This is a sketch that describes what occurred in the different stages of the Cuban war of liberation; but it has a content approximating the universal. Nevertheless, it will not always be possible to count on the degree of intimacy with the people, the conditions, and the leadership that existed in our war. It is unnecessary to say that Fidel Castro possesses the high qualities of a fighter and statesman: our path, our struggle, and our triumph we owed to his vision. We cannot say that without him the victory of the people would not have been achieved; but that victory would certainly have cost must more and would have been less complete.

CHAPTER III

ORGANIZATION OF THE GUERRILLA FRONT

1. SUPPLY

A good supply system is of basic importance to the guerrilla band. A group of men in contact with the soil must live from the products of this soil and at the same time must see that the livelihood continues of those who provide the supplies, the peasants; since in the hard guerrilla struggle it is not possible, above all at the beginning, for the group to dedicate its own energies to producing supplies, not to mention that these supplies would be easily discovered and destroyed by enemy forces in a territory likely to be completely penetrated by the action of repressive columns. Supply in the first stages is always internal.

As the guerrilla struggle develops, it will be necessary to arrange supply from outside the limits or territory of the combat. At the beginning the band lives solely on what the peasants have; it may be possible to reach a store occasionally to buy something, but never possible to have lines of supply, since there is no territory in which to establish them. The line of supply and the store of food are conditioned by the development of the guerrilla struggle.

The first task is to gain the absolute confidence of the inhabitants of the zone; and this confidence is won by a positive attitude toward their problems, by help and a constant program of orientation, by the defense of their interests and the punishment of all who attempt to take advantage of the chaotic moment in which they live in order to use pressure, dispossess the peasants, seize their harvests, etc. The line should be soft and hard at the same time: soft and with a spontaneous cooperation for all those who honestly sympathize with the revolutionary movement; hard upon those who are attacking it outright, fomenting dissensions, or simply communicating important information to the enemy army.

Little by little the territory will be cleared, and there will then be a greater ease of action. The fundamental principle that ought to prevail is that of paying always for all merchandise taken from a friend. This merchandise can consist of crops or of articles from commercial establishments. Many times they will be donated, but at other times the economic conditions of the peasantry prevent such donations. There are cases in which the necessities of warfare force the band to take needed food from stores without paying for it, simply because there is no money. In such cases the merchant ought always to be given a bond, a promissory note, something that certifies to the debt, "the bonds of hope" already described. It is better to use this method only with people who are outside the limits of the liberated territory, and in such cases to pay as soon as possible all or at least a part of the debt. When conditions have improved sufficiently to maintain a territory permanently free from the dominion of the opposing army, it is possible to set up collective plantings, where the peasants work the land for the benefit of the guerrilla army. In this way an adequate food supply of a permanent character is guaranteed.

If the number of volunteers for the guerrilla army is much greater than the number of arms, and political circumstances prevent these men from entering zones dominated by the enemy, the rebel army can put them to work directly on the land, harvesting crops; this guarantees supply and adds something to their record of service looking toward future promotion to the status of combatants. However, it is more advisable that the peasants themselves sow their own crops; this results in work performed more effectively, with more enthusiasm and skill. When conditions have ripened even more, it is possible, depending on the crops involved, to arrange purchases of entire harvests in such a way that they can remain in the field or in warehouses for the use of the army.

When agencies also charged with the duty of supplying the peasant population have been established, all food supplies will be concentrated in these agencies in order to facilitate a system of barter among the peasants, with the guerrilla army serving as intermediary.

If conditions continue to improve, taxes can be established; these should be as light as possible, above all for the small producer. It is important to pay attention to every detail of relations between the peasant class and the guerrilla army, which is an emanation of that class.

Taxes may be collected in money in some cases, or in the form of a part of the harvest, which will serve to increase the food supplies. Meat is one of the articles of primary necessity. Its production and conservation must be assured. Farms should be established under peasants having no apparent connection with the army, if the zone is not secure; they will devote themselves to the production of chickens, eggs, goats, and pigs, starting with stock that has been bought or confiscated from the large landowners. In the zones of big estates there are usually large quantities of cattle. These can be killed and salted and the meat maintained in condition for consumption for a long period of time.

This will also produce hides. A leather industry, more or less primitive, can be developed to provide leather for shoes, one of the fundamental accessories in the struggle. In general, necessary foods are the following (depending on the zone): meat, salt, vegetables, starches, or grains. The basic food is always produced by the peasants; it may be "malanga," as in the mountainous regions of Oriente Province in Cuba; it may be corn, as in the mountainous regions of Mexico, Central America, and Peru; potatoes, also in Peru; in other zones, such as Argentina, cattle; wheat in others; but always it is necessary to assure a supply of the fundamental food for the troop as well as some kinds of fat which permit better food preparation; these may be animal or vegetable fats.

Salt is one of the essential supplies. When the force is near the sea and in contact with it, small dryers should be established immediately; these will assure some production in order always to have a reserve stock and the ability to supply the troops. Remember that in wild places such as these, where only some of the foods are produced, it is easy for the enemy to establish an encirclement that can greatly hurt the flow of supplies to the zone. It is well to provide against such eventualities through peasant organization and civil organizations in general. The inhabitants of the zone should have on hand a minimum food supply that will permit them at least to survive, even though poorly, during the hardest phases of the struggle. An attempt should be made to collect rapidly a good provision of foods that do not decompose—such grains, for example, as corn, wheat, rice, etc., which will last quite a long time; also flour, salt, sugar, and canned goods of all types; further, the necessary seeds should be sown.

A moment will arrive when all the food problems of the troops in the zone are solved, but large quantities of other products will be needed: leather for shoes, if it has not been possible to create an industry for supplying the zone; cloth and all the accessory items necessary for clothing; paper, a press or mimeograph machine for newspapers, ink, and various other implements. In other words, the need for articles from the outside world will increase in the measure that the guerrilla bands become organized and the organization becomes more complex. In order for this need to be met adequately it is necessary that the organized lines of supply function perfectly. These organizations are composed basically of friendly peasants. They should have two poles, one in the guerrilla zone and one in a city. Departing and radiating from the guerrilla zones, lines of supply will penetrate the whole territory, permitting the passage of materials. Little by little the peasants accustom themselves to the danger (in small groups they can work marvels) and come to place the material that is needed in the indicated spot without running extreme risks. These movements can be carried out at night with mules or other similar transport animals or with trucks, depending on the zone. Thus, a very good supply may be achieved. This type of line of supply is for areas near places of operation.

It is also necessary to organize a line of supply from distant areas. These organizations should produce the money needed for making purchases and also the implements that cannot be produced in small towns or provincial cities. The organization will be nourished with direct donations from sectors sympathetic to the struggle, exchanged for secret "bonds," which should be delivered. A strict control over the personnel charged with the management of this operation should always be maintained. Serious consequences should follow any neglect of the indispensable moral requisites involved in this responsibility. Purchases can be made with cash and also with "bonds of hope" when the guerrilla army, having departed from its base of operations, menaces a new zone. In these cases there is no way to avoid taking the merchandise from any merchant; he must rely on the good faith and capabilities of the guerrilla armies to make good on his account.

For all lines of supply that pass through the country, it is necessary to have a series of houses, terminals, or way-stations, where supplies may be hidden during the day while waiting to be moved by night. These houses should be known only to those directly in charge of the food supplies. The least possible number of inhabitants should know about this transport operation, and these should be persons in whom the organization has the greatest confidence.

The mule is one of the most useful animals for these tasks. With an incredible resistance to fatigue and a capacity to walk in the hilliest zones, the mule can carry more than 100 kilograms on its back for many days. The simplicity of its food needs also makes it an ideal means of transport. The mule train should be well supplied with shoes; the muleteers should understand their animals and take the best possible care of them. In this way it is possible to have regular four-footed armies with an unbelievable utility. But frequently, despite the strength of the animal and its capacity to bear up through the hardest days, difficulty of passage will make it necessary to leave the cargo in fixed sites. In order to avoid this necessity, there should be a team charged with making trails for this class of animals. If all these conditions are met, if an adequate organization is created, and if the rebel army maintains excellent relations as needed with the peasants, an effective and lasting supply for the whole troop is guaranteed.

2. CIVIL ORGANIZATION

The civil organization of the insurrectional movement is very important on both fronts, the external and the internal. Naturally, these two have characteristics that are as different as their functions, though they both perform tasks that fall under the same name. The collections that can be carried out on the external front, for example, are not the same as those which can take place on the internal front; neither are the propaganda and the supply. Let us describe first the tasks on the internal front. Here we are dealing with a place dominated, relatively speaking, by the forces of liberation.

Also, it is to be supposed that the zone is adapted to guerrilla warfare, because when these conditions do not exist, when the guerrilla fighting is taking place in poorly adapted terrain, the guerrilla organization increases in extension but not in depth; it embraces new places, but it cannot arrive at an internal organization, since the whole zone is penetrated by the enemy. On the internal front we can have a series of organizations which perform specific functions for more efficiency in administration. In general, propaganda belongs directly to the army, but it also can be separated from the army if kept under its control. (This point is so important that we will treat it separately.) Collections are a function of the civil organization, as are the general tasks of organizing the peasants and workers, if these are present. Both of these classes should be governed by one council.

Raising supplies, as we explained in a previous chapter, can be carried out in various ways: through direct or indirect taxes, through direct or indirect donations, and through confiscations; all this goes to make up the large chapter on supplies for the guerrilla army.

Keep in mind that the zone ought by no means to be impoverished by the direct action of the rebel army, even though the latter will be responsible indirectly for the impoverishment that results from enemy encirclement, a fact that the adversary's propaganda will repeatedly point out. Precisely for this reason conflicts ought not to be created by direct causes. There ought not be, for example, any regulations that prevent the farmers of a zone in liberated territory from selling their products outside that territory, save in extreme and transitory circumstances and with a full explanation of these interruptions to the peasantry. Every act of the guerrilla army ought always to be accompanied by the propaganda necessary to explain the reasons for it. These reasons will generally be well understood by a peasantry that has sons, fathers, brothers, or relations within this army, which is, therefore, something of their own.

In view of the importance of relations with the peasants, it is necessary to create organizations that make regulations for them, organizations that exist not only within the liberated area, but also have connections in the adjacent areas. Precisely through these connections it is possible to penetrate a zone for a future enlargement of the guerrilla front. The peasants will sow the seed with oral and written propaganda, with accounts of life in the other zone, of the laws that have already been issued for the protection of the small peasant, of the spirit of sacrifice of the rebel army; in a word, they are creating the necessary atmosphere for helping the rebel troops.

The peasant organizations should also have connections of some type that will permit the channeling and sale of crops by the rebel army agencies in enemy territory through intermediaries more or less benevolent, more or less friendly to the peasant class. Joined with a devotion to the cause which brings the merchant to defy dangers in such cases, there also exists the devotion to money that leads him to take advantage of the opportunity to gain profits.

We have already spoken, in connection with supply problems, of the importance of the department of road construction. When the guerrilla band has achieved a certain level of development, it no longer wanders about through diverse regions without an encampment; it has centers that are more or less fixed. Routes should be established varying from small paths permitting the passage of a mule to good roads for trucks. In all this, the capacity of the organization of the rebel army must be kept in mind, as well as the offensive capacity of the enemy, who may destroy these constructions and even make use of roads built by his opponent to reach the encampments more easily. The fundamental rule should be that roads are for assisting supply in places where any other solution would be impossible; they should not be constructed except in circumstances where there is a virtual certainty that the position can be maintained against an attack by the adversary. Another exception would be roads built without great risk to facilitate communication between points that are not of vital importance.

Furthermore, other means of communication may be established. One of these that is extremely important is the telephone. This can be strung in the forest with the convenience that arises from using trees for posts. There is the advantage that they are not visible to the enemy from above. The telephone also presupposes a zone that the enemy cannot penetrate.

The council—or central department of justice, revolutionary laws, and administration—is one of the vital features of a guerrilla army fully constituted and with territory of its own. The council should be under the charge of an individual who knows the laws of the country; if he understands the necessities of the zone from a juridical point of view, this is better yet; he can proceed to prepare a series of decrees and regulations that help the peasant to normalize and institutionalize his life within the rebel zone.

For example, during our experience in the Cuban war we issued a penal code, a civil code, rules for supplying the peasantry and rules of the agrarian reform. Subsequently, the laws fixing qualifications of candidates in the elections that were to be held later throughout the country were established; also the Agrarian Reform Law of the Sierra Maestra. The council is likewise in charge of accounting operations for the guerrilla column or columns; it is responsible for handling money problems and at times intervenes directly in supply.

All these recommendations are flexible; they are based upon an experience in a certain place and are conditioned by its geography and history; they will be modified in different geographical, historical, and social situations.

In addition to the council, it is necessary to keep the general health of the zone in mind. This can be done by means of central military hospitals that should give the most complete assistance possible to the whole peasantry. Whether adequate medical treatment can be given will depend upon the stage reached by the revolution. Civil hospitals and civil health administration are united directly with the guerrilla army, and their functions are performed by officers and men of the army, who have the dual function of caring for the people and orienting them toward better health. The big health problems among people in these conditions are rooted in their total ignorance of elementary principles of hygiene. This aggravates their already precarious situation.

The collection of taxes, as I have already said, is also a function of the general council.

Warehouses are very important. As soon as a place is taken that is to serve as a base for the guerrilla band, warehouses should be established in the most orderly fashion possible. These will serve to assure a minimum care of merchandise and, most important, will provide the control needed for equalizing distribution and keeping it equitable at later times.

Functions are different on the external front both in quantity and in quality. For example, propaganda should be of a national, orienting type, explaining the victories obtained by the guerrilla band, calling workers and peasants to effective mass fights, and giving news, if there is any, of victories obtained on this front itself. Solicitation of funds is completely secret; it ought to be carried out with the greatest care possible, isolating small collectors in the chain completely from the treasurer of the organization.

This organization should be distributed in zones that complement each other in order to form a totality, zones that may be provinces, states, cities, villages, depending on the magnitude of the movement. In each of them there must be a finance commission that takes charge of the disposal of funds collected. It is possible to collect money by selling bonds or through direct donations. When the development of the struggle is more advanced, taxes may be collected; when industries come to recognize the great force that the insurrectional army possesses, they will consent to pay. Supply procurement should be fitted to the necessities of the guerrilla bands; it will be organized in the form of a chain of merchandise in such a way that the more common articles are procured in nearby places, and the things that are really scarce or impossible to procure locally, in larger centers. The effort always is to keep the chain as limited as possible, known to the smallest number of men; it can thus perform its mission for a longer time.

Sabotage should be directed by the civil organization in the external sector in coordination with the central command. In special circumstances, after careful analysis, assaults on persons will be used. In general we consider that this is not desirable except for the purpose of eliminating some figure who is notorious for his villainies against the people and the virulence of his repression. Our experience in the Cuban struggle shows that it would have been possible to save the lives of numerous fine comrades who were sacrificed in the performance of missions of small value. Several times these ended with enemy bullets of reprisal on combatants whose loss could not be compared with the results obtained. Assaults and terrorism in indiscriminate form should not be employed. More preferable is effort directed at large concentrations of people in whom the revolutionary idea can be planted and nurtured, so that at a critical moment they can be mobilized and with the help of the armed forces contribute to a favorable balance on the side of the revolution.

For this it is necessary also to make use of popular organizations of workers, professional people, and peasants, who work at sowing the seed of the revolution among their respective masses, explaining, providing revolutionary publications for reading, teaching the truth. One of the characteristics of revolutionary propaganda must be truth. Little by little, in this way, the masses will be won over. Those among them who do the best work may be chosen for incorporation into the rebel army or assignment to other tasks of great responsibility.

This is the outline of civil organization within and outside guerrilla territory at a time of popular struggle. There are possibilities of perfecting all these features to a high degree. I repeat once more, it is our Cuban experience which speaks through me; new experiences can vary and improve these concepts. We offer an outline, not a bible.

3. THE ROLE OF THE WOMAN

The part that the woman can play in the development of a revolutionary process is of extraordinary importance. It is well to emphasize this, since in all our countries, with their colonial mentality, there is a certain underestimation of the woman which becomes a real discrimination against her.

The woman is capable of performing the most difficult tasks, of fighting beside the men; and despite current belief, she does not create conflicts of a sexual type in the troops.

In the rigorous combatant life the woman is a companion who brings the qualities appropriate to her sex, but she can work the same as a man and she can fight; she is weaker, but no less resistant than he. She can perform every class of combat task that a man can at a given moment, and on certain occasions in the Cuban struggle she performed a relief role.

Naturally the combatant women are a minority. When the internal front is being consolidated and it is desirable to remove as many combatants as possible who do not possess indispensable physical characteristics, the women can be assigned a considerable number of specific occupations, of which one of the most important, perhaps the most important, is communication between different combatant forces, above all between those that are in enemy territory. The transport of objects, messages, or money, of small size and great importance, should be confided to women in whom the guerrilla army has absolute confidence; women can transport them using a thousand tricks; it is a fact that however brutal the repression, however thorough the searching, the woman receives a less harsh treatment than the man and can carry her message or other object of an important or confidential character to its destination.

As a simple messenger, either by word of mouth or of writing, the woman can always perform her task with more freedom than the man, attracting less attention and at the same time inspiring less fear of danger in the enemy soldier. He who commits brutalities acts frequently under the impulse of fear or apprehension that he himself will be attacked, since this is one form of action in guerrilla warfare.

Contacts between separated forces, messages to the exterior of the lines, even to the exterior of the country; also objects of considerable size, such as bullets, are transported by women in special belts worn beneath their skirts. But also in this stage a woman can perform her habitual tasks of peacetime; it is very pleasing to a soldier subjected to the extremely hard conditions of this life to be able to look forward to a seasoned meal which tastes like something. (One of the great tortures of the war was eating a cold, sticky, tasteless mess.) The woman as cook can greatly improve the diet and, furthermore, it is easier to keep her in these domestic tasks; one of the problems in guerrilla bands is that all works of a civilian character are scorned by those who perform them; they are constantly trying to get out of these tasks in order to enter into forces that are actively in combat.

A task of great importance for women is to teach beginning reading, including revolutionary theory, primarily to the peasants of the zone, but also to the revolutionary soldiers. The organization of schools, which is a part of the civil organization, should be done principally through women, who arouse more enthusiasm among children and enjoy more affection from the school community. Likewise, when the fronts have been consolidated and a rear exists, the functions of the social worker also fall to women who investigate the various economic and social evils of the zone with a view to changing them as far as possible.

The woman plays an important part in medical matters as nurse, and even as doctor, with a gentleness infinitely superior to that of her rude companion in arms, a gentleness that is so much appreciated at moments when a man is helpless, without comforts, perhaps suffering severe pain and exposed to the many dangers of all classes that are a part of this type of war.

Once the stage of creating small war industries has begun, the woman can also contribute here, especially in the manufacture of uniforms, a traditional employment of women in Latin American countries. With a simple sewing machine and a few patterns she can perform marvels. Women can take part in all lines of civil organization. They can replace men perfectly well and ought to do so, even where persons are needed for carrying weapons, though this is a rare accident in guerrilla life.

It is important to give adequate indoctrination to men and women, in order to avoid all kinds of misbehavior that can operate to hurt the morale of the troops; but persons who are otherwise free and who love each other should be permitted to marry in the Sierra and live as man and wife after complying with the simple requirements of the guerrilla band.

4. MEDICAL PROBLEMS

One of the grave problems that confronts the guerrilla fighter is exposure to the accidents of his life, especially to wounds and sicknesses, which are very frequent in guerrilla warfare. The doctor performs a function of extraordinary importance in the guerrilla band, not only in saving lives, in which many times his scientific intervention does not count because of the limited resources available to him; but also in the task of reinforcing the patient morally and making him feel that there is a person near him who is dedicated with all his force to minimizing his pains. He gives the wounded or sick the security of knowing that a person will remain at his side until he is cured or has passed danger.

The organization of hospitals depends largely upon the stage of development of the guerrilla band. Three fundamental types of hospital organization corresponding to various stages can be mentioned.

In this development we have a first, nomadic phase. In it the doctor, if there is one, travels constantly with his companions, is just another man; he will probably have to perform all the other functions of the guerrilla fighter, including that of fighting, and will suffer at times the depressing and desperate task of treating cases in which the means of saving life are not available. This is the stage in which the doctor has the most influence over the troops, the greatest importance for their morale. During this period in the development of the guerrilla band the doctor achieves to the full his character of a true priest who seems to carry in his scantily equipped knapsack needed consolation for the men. The value of a simple aspirin to one who is suffering is beyond calculation when it is given by the friendly hand of one who sympathetically makes the suffering his own. Therefore the doctor in the first stage should be a man who is totally identified with the ideals of the revolution, because his words will affect the troops much more deeply than those spoken by any other member.

In the normal course of events in guerrilla warfare another stage is reached that could be called "semi-nomadic." In it there are encampments, more or less frequented by the guerrilla troops; friendly houses of complete confidence where it is possible to store objects and even leave the wounded; and a growing tendency for the troop to become settled. At this stage the task of the doctor is less trying; he may have emergency surgical equipment in his knapsack and another more complete outfit for less urgent operations in a friendly house. It is possible to leave the sick and wounded in the care of peasants who will give their help with great devotion. He can also count on a larger number of medicines kept in convenient places; these should be completely catalogued as well as possible, considering the circumstances in which he lives. In this same semi-nomadic state, if the band operates in places that are absolutely inaccessible, hospitals can be established to which the sick and wounded will go for recovery.

In the third stage, when there are zones invulnerable to the enemy, a true hospital organization is constructed. In its most developed form, it can consist of three centers of different types. In the combat category there ought to be a doctor, the combatant the most loved by the troop, the man of battle, whose knowledge does not have to be too deep. I say this because his task is principally one of giving relief and of preparing the sick or wounded, while the real medical work is performed in hospitals more securely situated. A surgeon of quality ought not to be sacrificed in the line of fire.

When a man falls in the front line, stretcher-bearers, if these are available given the organization of the guerrilla band, will carry him to the first post; if they are not available, his companions themselves will perform this duty. Transport of the wounded in rough zones is one of the most delicate of all tasks and one of the most painful experiences in a soldier's life. Perhaps the transport of a wounded man is harder on all concerned, because of his sufferings and of the spirit of sacrifice in the troop, than the fact itself of being wounded, however grave it may be. The transport can be carried out in different ways according to the characteristics of the ground. In rough and wooded places, which are typical in guerrilla warfare, it is necessary to walk single file. Here the best system is to use a long pole, with the patient carried in a hammock that hangs from it.

The men take turns carrying the weight, one before and one behind. They should yield place to two other companions frequently, since the shoulders suffer severely and the individual gradually wears himself out carrying this delicate and heavy burden.

When the wounded soldier has passed through this first hospital, he then goes with the information as to what has been done for him to a second center, where there are surgeons and specialists depending upon the possibilities of the troop. Here the more serious operations needed for saving life or relieving individuals from danger are performed.

Afterwards, at a third level, hospitals with the greatest comforts possible are established for direct investigation in the zones affected of the causes and effects of illnesses that afflict the inhabitants of the area. These hospitals of the third group, which correspond to a sedentary life, are not only centers of convalescence and of operations of less urgency, but also establishments serving the civil population, where the hygienists perform their orienting function. Dispensaries that will permit an adequate individual surveillance should also be established. The hospitals of this third group can have, if the supply capability of the civil organization permits, a series of facilities that provide diagnosis even with laboratory and x-ray facilities.

Other useful individuals are the assistants to the doctor. They are generally youths with something of a vocation and some knowledge, with fairly strong physiques; they do not bear arms, sometimes because their vocation is medicine, but usually because there are insufficient arms for all who want them. These assistants will be in charge of carrying most of the medicines, an extra stretcher or hammock, if circumstances make this possible. They must take charge of the wounded in any battle that is fought.

The necessary medicines should be obtained through contacts with health organizations that exist in territory of the enemy. Sometimes they can be obtained from such organizations as the International Red Cross, but this possibility should not be counted upon, especially in the first moments of the struggle. It is necessary to organize an apparatus that will permit rapid transport of needed medicines in case of danger and that will gradually supply all the hospitals with the supplies needed for their work, military as well as civil. Also, contacts should be made in the surrounding areas with doctors who will be capable of helping the wounded whose cases are beyond the capacities or the facilities of the guerrilla band.

Doctors needed for this type of warfare are of different characteristics. The combatant doctor, the companion of men, is the type for the first stage; his functions develop as the action of the guerrilla band becomes more complicated and a series of connected organisms are constructed. General surgeons are the best acquisition for an army of this type. If an anesthetist is available, so much the better; though almost all operations are performed, not with gas anesthesia, but using "largactil" and sodium pentothal, which are much easier to administer and easier to procure and conserve. Besides general surgeons, bone specialists are very useful, because fractures occur frequently from accidents in the zone; they are also frequently caused by bullets producing this type of wound in limbs. The clinic serves the peasant mass mainly, since in general, sicknesses in the guerrilla armies are so easy of diagnosis as to be within the reach of anybody. The most difficult task is the cure of those produced by nutritional deficiencies.

In a more advanced stage there may even be laboratory technicians, if there are good hospitals, in order to have a complete outfit. Calls should be made to all sectors of the profession whose services are needed; it is quite likely that many will respond to this call and come to lend their help. Professionals of all classes are needed; surgeons are very useful, dentists as well. Dentists should be advised to come with a simple campaign apparatus and a campaign-type drill; working with this they can do practically everything necessary.

5. SABOTAGE

Sabotage is one of the invaluable arms of a people that fights in guerrilla form. Its organization falls under the civil or clandestine branch, since sabotage should be carried out, of course, only outside the territories dominated by the revolutionary army; but this organization should be directly commanded and oriented by the general staff of the guerrillas, which will be responsible for deciding the industries, communications, or other objectives that are to be attacked.

Sabotage has nothing to do with terrorism; terrorism and personal assaults are entirely different tactics. We sincerely believe that terrorism is of negative value, that it by no means produces the desired effects, that it can turn a people against a revolutionary movement, and that it can bring a loss of lives to its agents out of proportion to what it produces. On the other hand, attempts to take the lives of particular persons are to be made, though only in very special circumstances; this tactic should be used where it will eliminate a leader of the oppression. What ought never to be done is to employ specially trained, heroic, self-sacrificing human beings in eliminating a little assassin whose death can provoke the destruction in reprisal of all the revolutionaries employed and even more.

Sabotage should be of two types: sabotage on a national scale against determined objectives, and local sabotage against lines of combat. Sabotage on a national scale should be aimed principally at destroying communications. Each type of communication can be destroyed in a different way; all of them are vulnerable. For example, telegraph and telephone poles are easily destroyed by sawing them almost all the way through, so that at night they appear to be in normal condition; a sudden kick causes one pole to fall and this drags along with it all those that are weak, producing a blackout of considerable extent.

Bridges can be attacked with dynamite; if there is no dynamite, those made of steel can be made to fall very easily with an oxyacetylene blow torch. A steel truss bridge should be cut in its main beam and in the upper beam from which the bridge hangs. When these two beams have been cut at one end with the torch, they are then cut at the opposite end. The bridge will fall completely on one side and will be twisted and destroyed. This is the most effective way to knock out a steel bridge without dynamite. Railroads should also be destroyed, as should roads and culverts; at times trains should be blown up, if the power of the guerrilla band makes this possible.

The vital industries of each region at certain moments will also be destroyed by utilizing the necessary equipment. In these cases it is necessary to have an overall view of the problem and to be sure that a center of work is not destroyed unless the moment is decisive, since this brings with it as a consequence massive unemployment of workers and hunger. The enterprises belonging to the potentates of the regime should be eliminated (and attempts made to convince the workers of the need for doing so), unless this will bring very grave social consequences.

We reiterate the importance of sabotage against communications. The great strength of the enemy army against the rebels in the flatter zones is rapid communication; we must, then, constantly undermine that strength by knocking out railroad bridges, culverts, electric lights, telephones; also aqueducts and in general everything that is necessary for a normal and modern life.

Around the combat lines sabotage should be performed in the same way but with much more audacity, with much more dedication and frequency. Here it is possible to count on the invaluable aid of the flying patrols of the guerrilla army, which can descend into these zones and help the members of the civil organization perform a given task. Again, sabotage ought to be aimed principally at communications, but with much more persistence. All factories, all centers of production that are capable of giving the enemy something needed to maintain his offensive against the popular forces, ought also to be liquidated.

Emphasis should be placed on seizing merchandise, cutting supplies as much as possible, if necessary frightening the large landowners who want to sell their farm products, burning vehicles that travel along the roads, and using them to blockade the roads. It is expedient in every action of sabotage that frequent contact be made with the enemy army at points not far away, always following the system of hit and run. It is not necessary to put up a serious resistance, but simply to show the adversary that in the area where the sabotage has been carried out there are guerrilla forces disposed to fight. This forces him to take a large number of troops, to go with care, or not to go at all.

Thus, little by little, all the cities in the zone surrounding guerrilla operations will be paralyzed.

6. WAR INDUSTRY

Industries of war within the sector of the guerrilla army must be the product of a rather long evolution; they also depend upon control of territory in a geographic situation favorable for the guerrilla. At a time when there are liberated zones and when strict blockades are established by the enemy over all supplies, different departments will be organized as necessary, in the manner already described. There are two fundamental industries, of which one is the manufacture of shoes and leather goods. It is not possible for a troop to walk without shoes in wooded zones, hilly, with many rocks and thorns. It is very difficult to march without shoes in such conditions; only the natives, and not all of them, can do it. The rest must have shoes. The industry is divided into two parts, one for putting on half-soles and repairing damaged shoes; the other will be devoted to the manufacture of rough shoes. There should be a small but complete apparatus for making shoes; since this is a simple industry practiced by many people in such regions it is very easy to procure. Connected with the shoe repair works there ought always to be a shop making all classes of canvas and leather goods for use by the troop, such as cartridge belts and knapsacks. Although these articles are not vital, they contribute to comfort and give a feeling of autonomy, of adequate supply, and of self-reliance to the troop.

An armory is the other fundamental industry for the small internal organization of the guerrilla band.

This also has different functions: that of simple repair of damaged weapons, of rifles, and other available arms; the function of manufacturing certain types of combat arms that the inventiveness of the people will create; and the preparation of mines with various mechanisms. When conditions permit, equipment for the manufacture of powder may be added. If it is possible to manufacture the explosive as well as the percussion mechanisms in free territory, brilliant achievements can be scored in this category, which is a very important one, because communications by road can be completely paralyzed by the adequate employment of mines.

Another group of industries that has its importance will make iron and tin products. In the iron works will be centered all labor connected with the equipping of the mules, such as making their shoes. In the tin works the fabrication of plates and especially of canteens is important. A foundry can be joined with the tin works. By melting soft metals it is possible to make grenades, which with a special type of charge will contribute in an important way to the armament of the troop. There ought to be a technical team for general repair and construction work of varied types, the "service battery," as it is called in regular armies. With the guerrillas it would operate as such, taking care of all necessities, but without any vestige of the bureaucratic spirit.

Someone must be in charge of communications. He will have as his responsibility not only propaganda communications, such as radio directed toward the outside, but also telephones and roads of all types. He will use the civil organization as necessary in order to perform his duties effectively. Remember that we are in a period of war subject to attack by the enemy and that often many lives depend upon timely communication.

For accommodating the troop it is well to have

cigarette and cigar factories. The leaf can be bought in selected places and carried to free territory where the articles for consumption by the soldiers can be manufactured. An industry for preparing leather from hides is also of great importance. All these are simple enterprises that can operate quite well anywhere and are easy to establish in the guerrilla situation. The industry for making leather requires some small construction with cement; also it uses large amounts of salt; but it will be an enormous advantage to the shoe industry to have its own supply of raw material. Salt should be made in revolutionary territory and accumulated in large quantities. It is made by evaporating water of a high saline concentration. The sea is the best source, though there may be others. It is not necessary to purify it of other ingredients for purposes of consumption, though these give it a flavor that is disagreeable at first.

Meat should be conserved in the form of jerked beef, which is easy to prepare. This can save many lives among the troop in extreme situations. It can be conserved with salt in large barrels for a fairly long time, and it can then be eaten in any circumstances.

7. PROPAGANDA

The revolutionary idea should be diffused by means of appropriate media to the greatest depth possible. This requires complete equipment and an organization. This organization should be of two types which complement each other in covering the whole national area: for propaganda originating outside free territory, that is, from the national civil organization; and propaganda originating within, that is, from the base of the guerrilla army. In order to coordinate these two propagandas, the functions of which are strictly related, there should be a single director for the whole effort.

Propaganda of the national type from civil organizations outside free territory should be distributed in newspapers, bulletins, and proclamations. The most important newspapers will be devoted to general matters in the country and will inform the public exactly of the state of the guerrilla forces, observing always the fundamental principle that truth in the long run is the best policy. Besides these publications of general interest there must be others more specialized for different sectors of the population. A publication for the countryside should bring to the peasant class a message from their companions in all the free zones who have already felt the beneficial effects of the revolution; this strengthens the aspirations of the peasantry. A workers' newspaper will have similar characteristics, with the sole difference that it cannot always offer a message from the combatant part of that class, since it is likely that workers' organizations will not operate within the framework of guerrilla warfare until the last stages.

The great watchwords of the revolutionary movement, the watchword of a general strike at an opportune moment, of help to the rebel forces, of unity, etc., should be explained. Other periodicals can be published; for example, one explaining the tasks of those elements in the whole island which are not combatants but which nevertheless carry out diverse acts of sabotage, of attempts, etc. Within the organization there can be periodicals aimed at the enemy's soldiers; these will explain facts of which they are otherwise kept ignorant. News bulletins and proclamations about the movement are very useful.

The most effective propaganda is that which is prepared within the guerrilla zone. Priority will be given to the diffusion of ideas among natives of the zone, offering explanations of the theoretical significance of the insurrection, already known to them as a fact. In this zone there will also be peasant periodicals, the general organ of all the guerrilla forces, and bulletins and proclamations. There will also be the radio.

All problems should be discussed by radio—for example, the way to defend oneself from air attacks and location of the enemy forces, citing familiar names among them. Propaganda for the whole nation will use newspapers of the same type as those prepared outside free territory, but it can produce fresher and more exact news, reporting facts and battles that are extremely interesting to the reader. Information on international affairs will be confined almost exclusively to commentary on facts that are directly related to the struggle of liberation.

The propaganda that will be the most effective in spite of everything, that which will spread most freely over the whole national area to reach the reason and the sentiments of the people, is words over the radio. The radio is a factor of extraordinary importance. At moments when war fever is more or less palpitating in every one in a region or a country, the inspiring, burning word increases this fever and communicates it to every one of the future combatants. It explains, teaches, fires, and fixes the future positions of both friends and enemies. However, the radio should be ruled by the fundamental principle of popular propaganda, which is truth; it is preferable to tell the truth, small in its dimensions, than a large lie artfully embellished. On the radio news should be given, especially of battles, of encounters of all types, and assassinations committed by the repression; also, doctrinal orientations and practical lessons to the civil population; and, from time to time, speeches by the chiefs of the revolution. We consider it useful that the principal newspaper of the movement bear a name that recalls something great and unifying, perhaps a national hero or something similar. Also, it should explain in articles of depth where the armed movement is going. It ought to create a consciousness of the great national problems, besides offering sections of more lively interest for the reader.

8. INTELLIGENCE

"Know yourself and your adversary and you will be able to fight a hundred battles without a single disaster." This Chinese aphorism is as valuable for guerrilla warfare as a biblical psalm. Nothing gives more help to combatant forces than correct information. This arrives spontaneously from the local inhabitants, who will come to tell its friendly army, its allies, what is happening in various places; but in addition it should be completely systematized. As we saw, there should be a postal organization with necessary contacts both within and outside guerrilla zones for carrying messages and merchandise. An intelligence service also should be in direct contact with enemy fronts. Men and women, especially women, should infiltrate; they should be in permanent contact with soldiers and gradually discover what there is to be discovered. The system must be coordinated in such a way that crossing the enemy lines into the guerrilla camp can be carried out without mishap.

If this is well done with competent agents the insurgent camp will be able to sleep more quietly.

This intelligence will be concerned principally, as I have already said, with the front line of fire or the forward enemy encampments that are in contact with no man's land; but it ought also to develop in the same measure as the guerrilla band develops, increasing its depth of operation and its potential to foresee larger troop movements in the enemy rear. Though all inhabitants are intelligence agents for the guerrilla band in the places where it is dominant or makes incursions, it is wise to have persons especially assigned to this duty. The peasants, not accustomed to precise battle language, have a strong tendency to exaggerate, so their reports must be checked. As the spontaneous forms of popular collaboration are molded and organized, it is possible to use the intelligence apparatus not only as an extremely important auxiliary but also as a weapon of attack by using its personnel, for example, as "sowers of fear." Pretending to be on the side of the enemy soldiers, they sow fear and instability by spreading discouraging information. By knowing exactly the places where the enemy troop is going to attack, it is easy to avoid him or, when the time is ripe, to attack him at places where it is least expected. Mobility, the basic tactic, can be developed to the maximum.

9. TRAINING AND INDOCTRINATION

The fundamental training of the soldier of liberation is the life itself with the guerrilla band, and no one can be a chief who has not learned his difficult office in daily armed exercises. Life with some companions will teach something about the handling of arms, about principles of orientation, about the manner of treating the civil population, about fighting, etc.; but the precious time of the guerrilla band is not to be consumed in methodical teaching. This begins only when there is a large liberated area and a large number of persons are needed for carrying out a combat function. Schools for recruits will then be established.

These schools then perform a very important function. They are to form new soldiers from persons who have not passed through that excellent sieve of formidable privations, guerrilla combatant life. Other privations must be suffered at the outset to convert them into the truly chosen. After having passed through very difficult tests, they will arrive at incorporating themselves into the kingdom of an army that lives from day to day and leaves no traces of its path anywhere. They ought to perform physical exercises, mainly of two types: an agile gymnastic with training for war of a commando type, which demands agility in attack and withdrawal; and hikes that are hard and exhausting that will serve to toughen the recruit for this kind of existence. Above all, they should live in the open air. They should suffer all the inclemencies of the weather in close contact with nature, as the guerrilla band does.

The school for recruits must have workers who will take care of its supply needs. For this there should be cattle sheds, grain sheds, gardens, dairy, everything necessary, so that the school will not constitute a charge on the general budget of the guerrilla army. The students can serve in rotation in the work of supply, either as punishment for bad conduct or simply as volunteers. This will depend upon characteristics proper to the zone where the school is being held. We believe that a good principle is to assign volunteers and to cover the remaining work quotas with those who have the poorest conduct and show the poorest disposition for learning warfare.

The school should have its small medical organization with a doctor or nurse, according to the possibilities; this will provide the recruits with the best possible attention.

Shooting is the basic apprenticeship. The guerrilla fighter should be carefully trained in this respect, so that he will try to expend the least possible amount of ammunition. He begins by practicing what is called dry shooting. It consists of seating the rifle firmly on any kind of wooden apparatus as shown in

TARGET PRACTICE.

the picture. Without moving or firing the rifle the recruits direct the movement of a target until they think they have a hole at the center exactly in the line of sight. A mark is made on a backboard that remains stationary. If the mark for three tries gives a single point, this is excellent. When circumstances permit, practice with 22-calibre rifles will begin; this is very useful. If there is an excess of ammunition or a great need for preparing soldiers, opportunity will be given to fire with bullets.

One of the most important courses in the school for recruits, one which we hold to be basic and which can be given in any place in the world, is in meeting attack from the air. Our school had been positively identified from the air and received attacks once or twice daily. The form in which the students resisted the impact of these continuous bombardments on their regular places of instruction virtually showed which of the young men had possibilities for becoming useful soldiers in battle.

The important thing, that which must never be

neglected in a school for recruits, is indoctrination; this is important because the men arrive without a clear conception as to why they come, with nothing more than very diffuse concepts about liberty, freedom of the press, etc., without any clear foundation whatever. Therefore, the indoctrination should be carried out with maximum dedication and for the maximum amount of time possible. These courses should offer elementary notions about the history of the country, explained with a clear sense of the economic facts that motivate each of the historic acts; accounts of the national heroes and their manner of reacting when confronted with certain injustices; and afterwards an analysis of the national situation or of the situation in the zone. A short primer should be well studied by all members of the rebel army, so that it can serve as a skeleton of that which will come later.

There should also be a school for training teachers, where agreement can be reached on the choice of texts to be used, taking as a basis the contribution that each book can make to the educational process.

Reading should be encouraged at all times, with an effort to promote books that are worthwhile and that enlarge the recruit's facility to encounter the world of letters and great national problems. Further reading will follow as a vocation; the surrounding circumstances will awaken new desires for understanding in the soldiers. This result will be produced when, little by little, the recruits observe in their routine tasks the enormous advantages of men who have passed through the school over the remainder of the troop, their capacity for analyzing problems, their superior discipline, which is another of the fundamental things that the school should teach.

This discipline should be internal, not mechanical but justified by reasons and designed to produce formidable benefits in moments of combat.

10. THE ORGANIZATIONAL STRUCTURE OF THE ARMY OF A REVOLUTIONARY MOVEMENT

As we have seen, a revolutionary army of a guerrilla type, whatever its zone of operations, should also have a non-combatant organization for the performance of a series of extremely important auxiliary missions. We shall see later that this whole organization converges to lend the army maximum help, since obviously the armed fight is the crucial factor in the triumph.

The military organization is headed by a commander-in-chief, in the case of the Cuban experience by a comandante, who names the commanders of the different regions or zones; these latter have authority to govern their respective territories of action, to name column commanders, that is to say, the chiefs of each column, and the other lower officers.

Under the commander-in-chief there will be the zone commanders; under them several columns of varying size, each with a column commander; under the column commanders there will be captains and lieutenants, which, in our guerrilla organization, were the lowest grade. In other words, the first rank above the soldiers was the lieutenant.

This is not a model but a description of one reality, of how the organization worked in one country where it proved possible to achieve triumph over an army that was fairly well organized and armed. Even less here than in other respects is our experience a pattern. It simply shows how as events develop it is possible to organize an armed force. The ranks certainly have no importance, but it is important that no rank should be conferred that does not correspond to the effective battle force commanded. Ranks should not be given to persons who have not passed through the sieve of sacrifice and struggle, for that would conflict with morality and justice.

The description given above refers to a well-developed army, already capable of waging a serious combat. In the first stage of the guerrilla band, the chief can take the rank he likes, but he will still command only a small group of men.

One of the most important features of military organization is disciplinary punishment. Discipline must be one of the bases of action of the guerrilla forces (this must be repeated again and again). As we have already said, it should spring from a carefully reasoned internal conviction; this produces an individual with inner discipline. When this discipline is violated, it is necessary always to punish the offender, whatever his rank, and to punish him drastically in a way that hurts.

This is important, because pain is not felt by a guerrilla soldier in the same way as by a soldier of the regular army. The punishment of putting a soldier in jail for ten days constitutes for the guerrilla fighter a magnificent period of rest; ten days with nothing to do but eat, no marching, no work, no standing the customary guards, sleeping at will, resting, reading, etc. From this it can be deduced that deprivation of liberty ought not to be the only punishment available in the guerrilla situation.

When the combat morale of the individual is very high and self-respect strong, deprivation of his right to be armed can constitute a true punishment for the individual and provoke a positive reaction. In such cases, this is an expedient punishment.

The following painful incident is an example. During the battle for one of the cities of Las Villas province in the final days of the war, we found an individual asleep in a chair while others were attacking positions in the middle of the town. When questioned, the man responded that he was sleeping because he had been deprived of his weapon for firing accidentally. He was told that this was not the way to react to punishment and that he should regain his weapon, not in this way, but in the first line of combat.

A few days passed, and as the final assault on the city of Santa Clara began, we visited the first-aid hospital. A dying man there extended his hand, recalling the episode I have narrated, affirmed that he had been capable of recovering his weapon and had earned the right to carry it. Shortly afterwards, he died.

This was the grade of revolutionary morale that our troop achieved through the continual exercise of armed struggle. It is not possible to achieve it at the outset, when there are still many who are frightened, and subjective currents serve to put a brake on the influence of the Revolution; but finally it is reached through work and through the force of continual example.

Long night watches and forced marches can also serve as punishments; but the marches are not really practical, since they consume the individual to no purpose other than that of punishment, and they require guards who also wear themselves out. The guards suffer the further inconvenience of having to keep a watch on the persons being punished, who are soldiers of scant revolutionary mentality.

In the forces directly under my command I imposed the punishment of arrest with privation of sweets and cigarettes for light offenses and a total deprivation of food for worse offenses. The result was magnificent, even though the punishment was terrible; it is advisable only in very special circumstances.

APPENDICES

1. ORGANIZATION IN SECRET OF THE FIRST GUERRILLA BAND

Guerrilla warfare obeys laws, some derived from the general laws of war and others owing to its own special character. If there is a real intention to begin the struggle from some foreign country or from distant and remote regions within the same country, it is obvious that it must begin in small conspiratorial movements of secret members acting without mass support or knowledge. If the guerrilla movement is born spontaneously out of the reaction of a group of individuals to some form of coercion, it is possible that the later organization of this guerrilla nucleus to prevent its annihilation will be sufficient for a beginning. But generally guerrilla warfare starts from a well-considered act of will: some chief with prestige starts an uprising for the salvation of his people, beginning his work in difficult conditions in a foreign country.

Almost all the popular movements undertaken against dictators in recent times have suffered from the same fundamental fault of inadequate preparation. The rules of conspiracy, which demand extreme secrecy and caution, have not generally been observed. The governmental power of the country frequently knows in advance about the intentions of the group or groups, either through its secret service or from imprudent revelations or in some cases from outright declarations, as occurred, for example, in our case, in which the invasion was announced and summed up in the phrase of Fidel Castro: "In the year '56 we will be free or we will be martyrs."

Absolute secrecy, a total absence of information in the enemy's hands, should be the primary base of the movement. Secondly and also very important is selection of the human material. At times this selection can be carried out easily, but at others it will be extremely difficult, since it is necessary to rely on those elements that are available, long-time exiles or persons who present themselves when the call goes out simply because they understand that it is their duty to enroll in the battle to liberate their country, etc. There may not be the necessary facilities for making a complete investigation of these individuals. Nevertheless, even though elements of the enemy regime introduce themselves, it is unpardonable that they should later be able to pass information, because in the period just prior to an action all those who are going to participate should be concentrated in secret places known only to one or two persons; they should be under the strict vigilance of their chiefs and without the slightest contact with the outside world. Whenever there are concentrations, whether as a preparation for departure or in order to carry out preliminary training or simply to hide from the police, it is necessary always to keep all new personnel about whom there is no clear knowledge available away from the key places.

In underground conditions no one, absolutely no one, should know anything more than the strictly indispensable; and there ought not to be talk in front of anyone. When certain types of concentration have been carried out, it is necessary even to control letters that leave and arrive in order to have a total knowledge of the contacts that the individuals maintain; no one should be permitted to live alone, nor to go out alone; personal contacts of the future member of the liberating army, contacts of any type, should be prevented by every means. However positive the role of women in the struggle, it must be emphasized that they can also play a destructive part. The weakness for women that young men have when living apart from their habitual medium of life in special, even psychic conditions, is well known. As dictators are well aware of this weakness, they try to use it for infiltrating their spies. At times the relationship of these women with their superiors is clear and even notorious; at other times, it is extremely difficult to discover even the slightest evidence of contact; therefore, it is necessary also to prohibit relations with women.

The revolutionary in a clandestine situation preparing for war should be a complete ascetic; this also serves to test one of the qualities that later will be the basis of his authority, discipline. If an individual repeatedly disobeys orders of his superiors and makes contacts with women, contracts friendships that are not permitted, etc., he should be separated immediately, not merely because of the potential dangers in the contacts, but simply because of the violation of revolutionary discipline.

Unconditional help should not be expected from a government, whether friendly or simply negligent, that allows its territory to be used as a base of operations; one should regard the situation as if he were in a completely hostile camp. The few exceptions that of course can occur are really confirmations of the general rule.

We shall not speak here of the number of persons that should be readied. This depends upon so many and such varied conditions that it is practically impossible to specify. But the minimum number with which it is possible to initiate a guerrilla war can be mentioned. In my opinion, considering the normal desertions and weaknesses in spite of the rigorous process of selection, there should be a nucleus of 30 to 50 men; this figure is sufficient to initiate an armed fight in any country of the Americas with their conditions of favorable territory for operations, hunger for land, repeated attacks upon justice, etc.

Weapons, as has already been said, should be of the same type as those used by the enemy. Considering always that every government is in principle hostile to a guerrilla action being undertaken from its territory, the bands that prepare themselves should not be greater than approximately 50 to 100 men per unit. In other words, though there is no objection to 500 men initiating a war, all 500 should not be concentrated in one place. They are so numerous as to attract attention and in case of any betrayal of confidence or of any raid, the whole group falls; on the other hand, it is more difficult to raid various places simultaneously.

The central headquarters for meetings can be more or less known, and the exiled persons will go there to hold meetings of all types; but the leaders ought not to be present except very sporadically, and there should be no compromising documents. The leaders should use as many different houses as possible, those least likely to be under surveillance. Arms deposits should be distributed in several places, if possible; these should be an absolute secret, known to only one or two people.

Weapons should be delivered into the hands of those who are going to use them only when the war is about to be initiated. Thus a punitive action against persons who are training, while leading to their imprisonment, will not produce a loss of arms that are very difficult to procure. Popular forces are not in any condition to suffer such a loss.

Another important factor to which due attention must be given is preparation of the forces for the extremely hard fight that is going to follow. These forces should have a strict discipline, a high morale, and a clear comprehension of the task to be performed, without conceit, without illusions, without false hopes of an easy triumph. The struggle will be bitter and long, reverses will be suffered; they can be at the brink of annihilation; only high morale, discipline, faith in final victory, and exceptional leadership can save them. This was our Cuban experience; at one time twelve men were able to form the nucleus of the future army, because all these conditions were met and because the one who led us was named Fidel Castro.

Besides ideological and moral preparations, careful physical training is necessary. The guerrillas will, of course, select a mountainous or very wild zone for their operations. At any rate, in whatever situation they find themselves, the basic tactic of the guerrilla army is the march, and neither slow men nor tired men can be tolerated. Adequate training therefore includes exhausting hikes day and night, day after day, increasing gradually, always continued to the brink of exhaustion, with emulation used to increase speed. Resistance and speed will be fundamental qualities of the first guerrilla nucleus. Also a series of theoretical principles can be taught, for example, direction finding, reading, and forms of sabotage. If possible, there should be training with military rifles, frequent firing, above all at distant targets, and much instruction about the way to economize bullets.

To the guerrilla fighter, economy and utilization of ammunition down to the last bullet should be almost like religious tenets. If all these admonitions are followed, the guerrilla forces may well reach their goal.

2. DEFENSE OF POWER THAT HAS BEEN WON

Naturally victory cannot be considered as finally won until the army that sustained the former regime has been systematically and totally smashed. Further, all the institutions that sheltered the former regime should be wiped out. But since this is a manual for guerrilla bands we will confine ourselves to analyzing the problem of national defense in case of war or aggression against the new power.

The first development we meet is that world public opinion, "the respectable press," the "truthful" news agencies of the United States and of the other countries belonging to the monopolies will begin an attack on the liberated country, an attack as aggressive and systematic as the laws of popular reform. For this reason not even a skeleton of personnel from the former army can be retained. Militarism, mechanical obedience, traditional concepts of military duty, discipline and morale cannot be eradicated with one blow. Nor can the victors, who are good fighters, decent and kind-hearted, but at the same time generally lacking education, be allowed to remain in contact with the vanquished, who are proud of their specialized military knowledge in some combat arm—in mathematics, fortifications, logistics, etc.—and who hate the uncultured guerrilla fighters with all their might.

There are, of course, individual cases of military men who break with the past and enter into the new organization with a spirit of complete cooperation. These persons are doubly useful, because they unite with their love of the people's cause the knowledge necessary for carrying forward the creation of the new popular army. A second step will be consequent upon the first: as the old army is smashed and dismembered as an institution and its former posts occupied by the new army, it will be necessary to reorganize the new force. Its former guerrilla character, operating under independent chiefs without planning, can be changed; but it is very important to emphasize that operational concepts of the guerrilla band should still serve as the guide to structure. These concepts will determine the organic formation and the equipment of the popular army. Care should be taken to avoid the error that we fell into during the first months of trying to put the new popular army into the old bottles of military discipline and ancient organization. This error can cause serious maladjustments and can lead to a complete lack of organization.

Preparation should begin immediately for the new defensive war that will have to be fought by the people's army, accustomed to independence of command within the common struggle and dynamism in the management of each armed group. This army will have two immediate problems. One will be the incorporation of thousands of last-hour revolutionaries, good and bad, whom it is necessary to train for the rigors of guerrilla life and to give revolutionary indoctrination in accelerated and intensive courses. Revolutionary indoctrination that gives the necessary ideological unity to the army of the people is the basis of national security both in the long and short runs. The other problem is the difficulty of adaptation to the new organizational structure.

A corps to take charge of sowing the new truths of the Revolution among all the units of the army should immediately be created. It should explain to the soldiers, peasants, and workers, who have come out of the mass of the people, the justice and the truth of each revolutionary act, the aspirations of the Revolution, why there is a fight, why so many companions have died without seeing the victory. United to this intensive indoctrination, accelerated courses of primary instruction that will begin to overcome illiteracy should also be given, in order to improve the rebel army gradually until it has become an instrument of high technical qualifications, solid ideological structure, and magnificent combat power.

Time will create these three qualities. The military apparatus can continue to be perfected as time goes on; the former combatants can be given special courses to prepare them to serve as professional military men who will then give annual courses of instruction to the people joining voluntarily or by conscription. This will depend on national characteristics and rules cannot be stated.

From this point forward we are expressing the opinion of the command of the Rebel Army with respect to the policy to be followed in the concrete Cuban situation, given the menace of foreign invasion, the conditions of the modern world at the end of 1959 or the beginning of 1960, with the enemy in sight, analyzed, evaluated, and awaited without fear. In other words, we are no longer theorizing for the instruction of others about what has already been done; rather we theorize about what has been done by others in order to apply it ourselves in our own national defense.

As our problem is to theorize about the Cuban case, to locate and test our hypothesis on the map of American realities, we present as an epilogue the following analysis of the Cuban situation, its present and its future.

EPILOGUE

ANALYSIS OF THE CUBAN SITUATION, ITS PRESENT AND ITS FUTURE

A year has now passed since the flight of the dictator, the culmination of a long armed civil struggle by the Cuban people. The achievements of the government in the social, economic, and political fields are enormous; nevertheless, it is necessary to analyze them, to evaluate each act and to show precisely the dimensions of our Cuban Revolution. This national Revolution, fundamentally agrarian, having the enthusiastic support of workers, of people from the middle class and today even of owners of industry, has acquired a continental and world-wide importance, enhanced by its peculiar characteristics and by the inflexible will of the people.

It will not be possible to present a synthesis, however brief, of all the laws passed, all of them undoubtedly of popular benefit. It will be enough to select a few for special emphasis and to show at the same time the logical chain that carries us forward, step by step, in a progressive and necessary order of concern for the problems of the Cuban people.

The first alarm for the parasitic classes of the country is sounded in the rent law, the reduction of electric rates, and government intervention in the telephone company followed by a reduction in rates, all decreed in rapid succession. Those who had thought Fidel Castro and the men who made this Revolution to be nothing more than politicians of the old style, manageable simpletons with beards their only distinction, now began to suspect that something deeper was emerging from the bosom of the Cuban people and that their privileges were in danger. The word "Communism" began to envelop the figures of the leaders and of the triumphant guerrilla fighters; consequently the word anti-Communism, as the position dialectically opposed, began to serve as a nucleus for all those who resented the loss of their unjust privileges.

The law on vacant lots and the law on installment sales aggravated this sensation of malaise among the usurious capitalists. But these were minor skirmishes with the reactionaries; everything was still all right and possible. "This crazy fellow," Fidel Castro, could be counseled and guided to good paths, to good "democratic" paths, by a Dubois or a Porter. It was necessary to place hope in the future.

The Agrarian Reform law was a tremendous jolt. Most of those who had been hurt now saw clearly. One of the first was Gaston Baquero, the voice of reaction; he had accurately interpreted what was going to happen and had retired to quieter scenes under the Spanish dictatorship. There were still some who thought that "the law is the law," that other governments had already promulgated such laws, theoretically designed to help the people. Carrying out these laws was another thing. That brash and complex child that had the initials INRA for its familiar name was treated at the beginning with peevish and touching paternalism within the ivory towers of learning, pervaded with social doctrines and respectable theories of public finance, to which the uncultivated and absurd mentalities of the guerrilla fighters could not arrive. But INRA advanced like a tractor or a war tank, because it is tractor and tank at the same time, breaking down the walls of the great estates as it passed and creating new social relations in the ownership of land. This Cuban Agrarian Reform appeared with various characteristics important for America. It was anti-feudal in the sense that it eliminated the Cuban-style latifundia, annulled all contracts that called for payment of rent of land in crops, and liquidated the servile relations that existed principally in coffee and tobacco production, two important branches of our agriculture. But it also was an Agrarian Reform in a capitalist medium to destroy the pressure of monopoly on human beings, isolated or joined together, to help them work their land honorably and to produce without fear of the creditor or the master. It had the characteristic from the first moment of assuring to peasants and agricultural workers, those who give themselves to the soil, needed technical help from competent personnel; machinery; financial help provided through credits from INRA or para-state banks; and big help from the "Association of People's Stores" that has developed on a large scale in Oriente and is in process of development in other provinces. The state stores, replacing the old usurers, provide just financing and pay a just price for the harvest.

Compared with the other three great agrarian reforms in America (Mexico, Guatemala, and Bolivia) the most important distinctive characteristic is the decision to carry Cuban reform all the way, without concessions or exceptions of any kind. This total Agrarian Reform respects no rights that are not rights of the people nor singles out any class or nationality for discriminatory treatment: the force of the law falls equally on the United Fruit Company and on the King Ranch, as on the big Cuban landowners.

Under these conditions land is being cleared,

mainly for the production of crops which are very important to the country, rice, oil-producing grains and cotton; these are being intensively developed. But the nation is not satisfied and is going to recover all its stolen resources. Its rich sub-soil, which has been a field of monopolist voracity and struggle, is virtually recovered by the petroleum law. This law, like the Agrarian Reform and all the others promulgated by the Revolution, responds to Cuba's irresistible necessities, to urgent demands of a people that wishes to be free, that wishes to be master of its economy, that wishes to prosper and to reach ever higher goals of social development. But for this very reason it is an example for the continent and feared by the oil monopolies. It is not that Cuba directly hurts the petroleum monopoly substantially. There is no reason to believe the country to be rich in reserves of the prized fuel, even though there are reasonable hopes of obtaining a supply that will satisfy its internal needs. On the other hand, by its law Cuba gives a palpable example to the brother peoples of America, many of them foraged by these monopolies or pushed into intercine wars in order to satisfy the necessities or appetites of competing trusts. At the same time Cuba shows the possibility of acting in America and the exact hour when action ought to be considered. The great monopolies also cast their worried look upon Cuba; not only has someone in the little island of the Caribbean dared to liquidate the interests of the omnipotent United Fruit Company, legacy of Mr. Foster Dulles to his heirs; but also the empires of Mr. Rockefeller and the Deutsch group have suffered under the lash of intervention by the popular Cuban Revolution.

This law, like the mining law, is the response of the people to those who try to check them with threats of force, with aerial incursions, with punishments of whatever type. Some say that the mining law is as important as the Agrarian Reform. We do not consider that it has this importance for the economy of the country in general, but it introduces another new feature: a 25 percent tax on the amount of product exported, to be paid by companies that sell our minerals abroad (leaving now something more than a hole in our territory). This not only contributes to our Cuban welfare; it also increases the relative strength of the Canadian monopolies in their struggle with the present exploiters of our nickel. Thus the Cuban Revolution liquidates the latifundia, limits the profits of the foreign monopolies, limits the profits of the foreign intermediaries that dedicate themselves with parasitic capital to the commerce of importation, launches upon the world a new policy in America, dares to break the monopolist status of the giants of mining, and leaves one of them in difficulty, to say the least. This signifies a powerful new message to the neighbors of the great stronghold of monopoly, and causes repercussions throughout America. The Cuban Revolution breaks all the barriers of the news syndicates and diffuses its truth like a shower of dust among the American masses anxious for a better life. Cuba is the symbol of nationality renewed and Fidel Castro the symbol of liberation.

By a simple law of gravity the little island of one hundred fourteen thousand square kilometers and six and one-half million inhabitants assumes the leadership in the anticolonial struggle in America, in which serious handicaps in other countries permit Cuba to take the heroic, glorious and dangerous advanced post. The economically less weak nations of colonial America, the ones in which national capitalism develops haltingly in a continuous, relentless, and at times violent struggle against the foreign monopolies, now cede their place gradually to this small, new champion of liberty, since their governments do not have sufficient force to carry the fight forward. This is not a simple task, nor is it free from danger and difficulties. The backing of a whole people and an enormous charge of idealism and spirit of sacrifice are needed in the nearly solitary conditions in which we are carrying it out in America. Small countries have tried to maintain this post before Guatemala, the Guatemala of Quetzal, that dies when it is imprisoned in a cage, the Guatamala of the Indian Tecum Umam, fell before the direct aggression of the colonialists. Bolivia, the country of Morillo, the proto-martyr of American independence, yielded to the terrible hardships of the struggle after setting three examples that served as the foundation of the Cuban Revolution: the suppression of the army, agrarian reform, and nationalization of mines—maximum source of riches and at the same time maximum source of tragedy.

Cuba knows about these previous examples, knows the failures and the difficulties, but it knows also that we are at the dawning of a new era in the world. The pillars of colonialism have been swept aside by the power of the national and popular struggle in Asia and Africa. Solidarity among peoples does not now come from religion, customs, tastes, racial affinity or its lack. It arises from a similarity in economic and social conditions and from a similarity in desire for progress and recuperation. Asia and Africa joined hands in Bandung; Asia and Africa come to join hands with colonial and indigenous America through Cuba, in Havana.

On the other hand, the great colonial powers have lost ground before the struggle of the peoples. Belgium and Holland are two caricatures of empires; Germany and Italy lost their colonies. France is bitterly fighting a war that is lost. England, diplomatic and skillful, liquidates political power while maintaining the economic connections.

American capitalism replaced some of the old colonial capitalisms in the countries that began their independent life. But it knows that this is transitory and that there is no real security for its financial speculations in these new territories. The octopus cannot there apply its suckers firmly. The claw of the imperial eagle is trimmed. Colonialism is dead or is dying a natural death in all these places.

America is something else. It has been some time since the English lion with its voracious appetite departed from our America and the young and charming Yankee capitalists installed the "democratic" version of the English clubs, imposing their sovereign domination over every one of the twenty republics.

This is the colonial realm of North American monopoly, its reason for being and last hope, the "backyard of its own house." If all the Latin American peoples should raise the flag of dignity, as Cuba has done, monopoly would tremble; it would have to accommodate to a new political-economic situation and to substantial prunings of profits. Monopoly does not like profits to be pruned, and the Cuban example, this "bad example" of national and international dignity, is gaining strength in the countries of America. Each time that an impudent people cries out for liberation, Cuba is accused; and it is true in a sense that Cuba is guilty, because Cuba has shown the way, the way of the armed popular fight against armies supposed to be invincible, the way of struggle in wild places to wear down and destroy the enemy far from his bases, in a word, the way of dignity.

This Cuban example is bad, a very bad example, and monopoly cannot sleep quietly while this bad example remains at its feet, defying danger, advancing toward the future. It must be destroyed, voices declare. It is necessary to intervene in this bastion of "Communism," cry the servants of monopoly disguised as representatives in Congress. "The Cuban situation is very disturbing," say the artful defenders of the trusts; we all know that their meaning is: "It must be destroyed."

Very well. What are the different possibilities of aggressive action to destroy the bad example? One could be called the purely economic. This begins with a restriction on credit by North American banks and suppliers to all businessmen, national banks, and even the National Bank of Cuba. Credit is thus restricted in North America, and through the medium of associates an attempt is made to have the same policy adopted in all the countries of Western Europe; but this alone is not sufficient.

The denial of credits strikes a first strong blow at the economy, but recovery is rapid and the commercial balance evens out, since the victimized country is accustomed to living as best it can. It is necessary to apply more pressure. The sugar quota is brought into the picture: yes, no, no, yes. Hurriedly the calculating machines of the agents of monopoly total up all sorts of accounts and arrive at the final conclusion: it is very dangerous to reduce the Cuban quota and impossible to cancel it. Why very dangerous? Because besides being bad politics, it would awaken the appetite of ten or fifteen other supplier countries, causing them tremendous discomfort, because they would all consider they had a right to something more. It is impossible to cancel the quota, because Cuba is the largest, most efficient, and cheapest provider of sugar to the United States, and because sixty percent of the interests that profit directly from the production and commerce in sugar are United States interests. Besides, the commercial balance is favorable to the United States; whoever does not sell cannot buy; and it would set a bad example to break a treaty. Further, the supposed North American gift of paying nearly three cents above the market price is only the result of North American incapacity to produce sugar cheaply. The high wages and the low productivity of the soil prevent the Great Power from producing sugar at Cuban prices; and by paying this higher price for a product, they are able to impose burdensome treaties on all beneficiaries, not only Cuba. Impossible to liquidate the Cuban quota.

We do not consider likely the possibility that monopolists are employing a variant of the economic approach in bombarding and burning sugar cane fields, hoping to cause a scarcity of the product. Rather this appears to be a measure calculated to weaken confidence in the power of the revolutionary government. (The corpse of the North American mercenary stains more than a Cuban house with blood; it also stains a policy.[6] And what is to be said of the gigantic explosion of arms destined for the Rebel Army? [7])

Another vulnerable place where the Cuban economy can be squeezed is the supply of raw materials, such as cotton. However, it is well known that there is an over-production of cotton in the world, and any difficulty of this type would be transitory. Fuel? This is worth some attention; it is possible to paralyze a country by depriving it of fuel, and Cuba produces very little petroleum. It has some heavy fuel that can be used to operate its steam-driven machinery and some alcohol that can be used in vehicles; also, there are large amounts of petroleum in the world. Egypt can sell it, the Soviet Union can sell it, perhaps Iraq will be able to sell it shortly. It is not possible to develop a purely economic strategy.

As another possibility of aggression, if to this economic variant were added an intervention by some puppet power, the Dominican Republic, for example,

[6] A plane was damaged by the explosion of its own bomb dropped on Cuban territory. It crashed into a house, killing the pilot, who was an American. He carried charts showing that the plane had taken off from a field in Florida. The United States Government apologized.

[7] On March 4, 1960, a Belgian ship, *La Coubré,* loaded with ammunition for the Cuban armed forces, exploded in Havana harbor, killing approximately 100 persons. The cause of the explosion has never been established.

it would be somewhat more of a nuisance; but the United Nations would doubtless intervene, with nothing concrete having been achieved.

Incidentally, the new course taken by the Organization of American States creates a dangerous precedent of intervention. Behind the shield of the Trujillo pretext, monopoly solaces itself by constructing a means of aggression. It is sad that the Venezuelan democracy has put us in the difficult position of having to oppose an intervention against Trujillo. What a good turn it has done the pirates of the continent!

Among the new possibilities of aggression is physical elimination by means of an assault on the old "crazy fellow," Fidel Castro, who has become by now the focus of the monopolies' wrath. Naturally, measures must be arranged so that the other two dangerous "international agents," Raul Castro and the author, are also eliminated. This solution is appealing; if simultaneous assaults on all three or at least on the directing head succeeded, it would be a boon to the reaction. (But do not forget the people, Messrs. Monopolists and agents, the omnipotent people who in their fury at such a crime would crush and erase all those who had anything to do directly or indirectly with an assault on any of the chiefs of the Revolution; it would be impossible to restrain them.)

Another aspect of the Guatemalan variant is to put pressure on the suppliers of arms, in order to force Cuba to buy in Communist countries and then use this as an occasion to let loose another shower of insults. This could give results. "It may be," someone in our government has said, "that they will attack us as Communists, but they are not going to eliminate us as imbeciles."

Thus it begins to appear as if a direct aggression on the part of the monopolies will be necessary; various possible forms are being shuffled and studied in the IBM machines with all processes calculated. It occurs to us at the moment that the Spanish variant could be used. The Spanish variant would be one in which some initial pretext is seized upon for an attack by exiles with the help of volunteers, volunteers who would be mercenaries of course, or simply the troops of a foreign power, well supported by navy and air, well enough supported, shall we say, to be successful. It could also begin as a direct aggression by some state such as the Dominican Republic, which would send some of its men, our brothers, and many mercenaries to die on these beaches in order to provoke war; this would prompt the pure-intentioned monopolists to say that they do not wish to intervene in this "disastrous" struggle between brothers; they will merely limit and confine and freeze the war within its present limits by maintaining vigilance over the skies and seas of this part of America with cruisers, battleships, destroyers, aircraft carriers, submarines, minesweepers, torpedo boats, and airplanes. And it could happen that while these zealous guardians of continental peace were not allowing a single boat to pass with things for Cuba, some, many, or all of the boats headed for the unhappy country of Trujillo would escape the iron vigilance. Also they might intervene through some "reputable" inter-American organ, to put an end to the "foolish war" that "Communism" had unleashed in our island; or, if this mechanism of the "reputable" American organ did not serve, they might intervene directly, as in Korea, using the name of the international organ in order to restore peace and protect the interests of all nations.

Perhaps the first step in the aggression will not be against us, but against the constitutional government of Venezuela, in order to liquidate our last point of support on the continent. If this happens, it is possible that the center of the struggle against colonialism will move from Cuba to the great country of Bolivar. The people of Venezuela will rise to defend their liberties with all the enthusiasm of those who know that they are fighting a decisive battle, that behind defeat lies the darkest tyranny and behind victory the certain future of America. A stream of popular struggles can disturb the peace of the monopolist cemeteries formed out of our subjugated sister republics.

Many reasons argue against the chance of enemy victory, but there are two fundamental ones. The first is external: this is the year 1960, the year that will finally hear the voices of the millions of beings who do not have the luck to be governed by the possessors of the means of death and payment. Further, and this is an even more powerful reason, an army of six million Cubans will grasp weapons as a single man in order to defend its territory and its Revolution. Cuba will be a battlefield where the army will be nothing other than part of the people in arms. After destruction in a frontal war, hundreds of guerrilla bands under a dynamic command and a single center of orientation, will fight the battle all over the country. In cities the workers will die in their factories or centers of work, and in the country the peasants will deal out death to the invader from behind every palm tree and from every furrow of the new mechanically plowed field that the Revolution has given them.

And around the world international solidarity will create a barrier of hundreds of millions of people protesting against aggression. Monopoly will see how its pillars are undermined and how the spider web curtain of its newspaper lies is swept away by a puff. But let us suppose that they dare to defy the popular indignation of the world; what will happen here within?

The first thing to be noted, given our position as an easily vulnerable island without heavy arms, with a very weak air force and navy, is the necessity of applying the guerrilla concept to the fight for national defense.

Our ground units will fight with the fervor, decision, and enthusiasm of which the sons of the Cuban Revolution are capable in these glorious years of our history. But if the worst occurs, we are prepared to continue fighting even after the destruction of our army organization in a frontal combat. In other words, confronting large concentrations of enemy forces that succeed in destroying ours, we would change immediately into a guerrilla army with a good sense of mobility, with unlimited authority in our column commanders, though with a central command located somewhere in the country giving the necessary direction and fixing the general overall strategy.

The mountains would be the last line of defense of the organized armed vanguard of the people, which is the Rebel Army; but in every house of the people, on every road, in every forest, in every piece of national territory the struggle would be fought by the great army of the rearguard, the entire people trained and armed in the manner now to be described.

Since our infantry units will not have heavy arms, they will concentrate on anti-tank and anti-air defense. Mines in very large numbers, bazookas or anti-tank grenades, anti-aircraft cannon of great mobility and mortar batteries will be the only arms of any great power. The veteran infantry soldier, though equipped with automatic weapons, will know the value of ammunition. He will guard it with loving care. Special installations for reloading shells will accompany each unit of the army, maintaining reserves of ammunition even though precariously.

The air force will probably be badly hurt in the first moments of an invasion of this type. We are basing our calculations upon an invasion by a first-class foreign power or by a mercenary army of some other power, helped either openly or surreptitiously by this great power of first magnitude. The national air force, as I said, will be destroyed, or almost destroyed; only reconnaissance or liaison planes will remain, especially helicopters for minor functions.

The navy will also be organized for this mobile strategy; small launches will give the smallest target to the enemy and maintain maximum mobility. The great desperation of the enemy army in this case as before will be to find something to receive his blows. Instead he will find a gelatinous mass, in movement, impenetrable, that retreats and never presents a solid front, though it inflicts wounds from every side.

It is not easy to overcome an army of the people that is prepared to continue being an army in spite of its defeat in a frontal battle. Two great masses of the people are united around it: the peasants and the workers. The peasants have already given evidence of their efficiency in detaining the small band that was marauding in Pinar del Rio. These peasants will be trained principally in their own regions; but the platoon commanders and the superior officers will be trained, as is now already being done, in our military bases. From there they will be distributed throughout the thirty zones of agrarian development that form the new geographical division of the country. This will constitute thirty more centers of peasant struggle, charged with defending to the maximum their lands, their social conquests, their new houses, their canals, their dams, their flowering harvests, their independence, in a word, their right to live.

At the beginning they will oppose also a firm resistance to any enemy advance, but if this proves too strong for them, they will disperse, each peasant becoming a peaceful cultivator of his soil during the day and a fearsome guerrilla fighter at night, scourge of the enemy forces. Something similar will take place among the workers; the best among them will be trained also to serve thereafter as chiefs of their companions, teaching them principles of defense. Each social class, however, will have different tasks. The peasant will fight a battle typical of the guerrilla fighter; he should learn to be a good shot, to take advantage of all the difficulties of the ground and to disappear without ever showing his face. The workers, on the other hand, have the advantage of being within a modern city, which is a large and efficient fortress; at the same time their lack of mobility is a drawback. The worker will learn first to block the streets with barricades of any available vehicle, furniture, or utensil; to use every block as a fortress with communications formed by holes made in interior walls; to use that terrible arm of defense, the "Molotov cocktail"; and to coordinate his fire from the innumerable loopholes provided by the houses of a modern city.

From the worker masses assisted by the national police and those armed forces charged with the defense of the city, a powerful block of the army will be formed; but it must expect to suffer great losses. The struggle in the cities in these conditions cannot achieve the facility and flexibility of the struggle in the countryside: many will fall, including many leaders, in this popular struggle. The enemy will use tanks that will be destroyed rapidly as soon as the people learn their weaknesses and not to fear them; but before that the tanks will leave their balance of victims.

There will also be other organizations related to those of workers and peasants: first, the student militias, which will contain the flower of the student youth, directed and coordinated by the Rebel Army; organizations of youth in general, who will participate in the same way; and organizations of women, who will provide an enormous encouragement by their presence and who will do such auxiliary tasks for their companions in the struggle as cooking, taking care of the wounded, giving final comfort to those who are dying, doing laundry, in a word, showing their companions-in-arms that they will never be absent in the difficult moments of the Revolution. All this is achieved by wide-scale organization of the masses supplemented with patient and careful education, an education that begins and is confirmed in knowledge acquired from their own experience; it should concentrate on reasoned and true explanations of the facts of the Revolution.

The revolutionary laws should be discussed, explained, studied in every meeting, in every assembly, wherever the leaders of the Revolution are present for any purpose. Also, the speeches of the leaders, and in our case particularly of the undisputed leader, should constantly be read, commented upon, and discussed. People should come together in the country to listen by radio, and where there are more advanced facilities, to watch by television these magnificent popular lessons that our Prime Minister gives.

The participation of the people in politics, that is to say, in the expression of their own desires made into laws, decrees, and resolutions, should be constant. Vigilance against any manifestations opposed to the Revolution should also be constant; and vigilance over morale within the revolutionary masses should be stricter, if this is possible, than vigilance against the non-revolutionary or the disaffected. It can never be permitted, lest the Revolution take the dangerous path of opportunism, that a revolutionary of any category should be excused for grave offenses against decorum or morality simply because he is a revolutionary. The record of his former services may provide extenuating circumstances and they can always be considered in deciding upon the punishment, but the act itself must always be punished.

Respect for work, above all for collective work and work for collective ends, ought to be cultivated. Volunteer brigades to construct roads, bridges, docks or dams, and school cities should receive a strong impulse; these serve to forge a unity among persons showing their love for the Revolution with works.

An army that is linked in such ways with the people, that feels this intimacy with the peasants and the workers from which it emerged, that knows besides all the special techniques of its warfare and is psychologically prepared for the worst contingencies, is invincible; and it will be even more invincible as it makes the just phrase of our immortal Camilo a part of the flesh of the army and the citizenry: "The army is the people in uniform." Therefore, for all these reasons, despite the necessity that monopoly suppress the "bad example" of Cuba, our future is brighter than ever.

SOURCE: *Guerrilla Warfare*, trans. J. P. Morray (New York: Monthly Review, 1961).

GUERRILLA WARFARE: A METHOD (1963)

GUERRILLA WARFARE: A METHOD

Guerrilla warfare has been employed on innumerable occasions throughout history in different circumstances to obtain different objectives. Lately it has been employed in various popular wars of liberation when the vanguard of the people chose the road of irregular armed struggle against enemies of superior military power. Asia, Africa, and Latin America have been the scene of such actions in attempts to obtain power in the struggle against feudal, neo-colonial, or colonial exploitation. In Europe, guerrilla units were used as a supplement to native or allied regular armies.

In America, guerrilla warfare has been employed on several occasions. As a case in point, we have the experience of César Augusto Sandino fighting against the Yankee expeditionary force on the Segovia of Nicaragua. Recently we had Cuba's revolutionary war. Since then in America the problem of guerrilla war has been raised in discussions of theory by the progressive parties of the continent with the question of whether its utilization is possible or convenient. This has become the topic of very controversial polemics.

This article will express our views on guerrilla warfare and its correct utilization. Above all, we must emphasize at the outset that this form of struggle is a means to an end. That end, essential and inevitable for any revolutionary, is the conquest of political power. Therefore, in the analysis of specific situations in different countries of America, we must use the concept of guerrilla warfare in the limited sense of a method of struggle in order to gain that end.

Almost immediately the question arises: Is guerrilla warfare the only formula for seizing power in all of Latin America? Or, at any rate, will it be the predominant form? Or simply, will it be one formula among many used during the struggle? And ultimately we may ask: Will Cuba's example be applicable to the present situation on the continent? In the course of polemics, those who want to undertake guerrilla warfare are criticized for forgetting mass struggle, implying that guerrilla warfare and mass struggle are opposed to each other. We reject this implication, for guerrilla warfare is a people's war; to attempt to carry out this type of war without the population's support is the prelude to inevitable disaster. The guerrilla is the combat vanguard of the people, situated in a specified place in a certain region, armed and willing to carry out a series of warlike actions for the one possible strategic end—the seizure of power. The guerrilla is supported by the peasant and worker masses of the region and of the whole territory in which it acts. Without these prerequisites, guerrilla warfare is not possible.

> We consider that the Cuban Revolution made three fundamental contributions to the laws of the revolutionary movement in the current situation in America. First, people's forces can win a war against the army. Second, one need not always wait for all conditions favorable to revolution to be present; the insurrection itself can create them. Third, in the underdeveloped parts of America, the battleground for armed struggle should in the main be the countryside. (*Guerrilla Warfare*)

Such are the contributions to the development of the revolutionary struggle in America, and they can be applied to any of the countries on our continent where guerrilla warfare may develop.

The Second Declaration of Havana points out,

> In our countries two circumstances are joined: underdeveloped industry and an agrarian system of feudal character. That is why no matter how hard the living conditions of the urban workers are, the

rural population lives under even more horrible conditions of oppression and exploitation. But, with few exceptions, it also constitutes the absolute majority, sometimes more than 70 percent of the Latin American population.

Not counting the landlords who often live in the cities, this great mass earns its livelihood by working as peons on plantations earning miserable wages. Or they till the soil under conditions of exploitation no different than those of the Middle Ages. These circumstances determine in Latin America that the poor rural population constitutes a tremendous potential revolutionary force.

The armies are set up and equipped for conventional warfare. They are the force whereby the power of the exploiting classes is maintained. When they are confronted with the irregular warfare of peasants based on their home ground, they become absolutely powerless; they lose ten men for every revolutionary fighter who falls. Demoralization among them mounts rapidly when they are beset by an invisible and invincible army which provides them no chance to display their military academy tactics and their military fanfare, of which they boast so much, to repress the city workers and students.

The initial struggle of small fighting units is constantly nurtured by new forces; the mass movement begins to grow bold, the old order bit by bit breaks into a thousand pieces, and that is when the working class and the urban masses decide the battle.

What is it that from the very beginning of the fight makes those units invincible, regardless of the number, strength, and resources of their enemies? It is the people's support, and they can count on an ever-increasing mass support.

But the peasantry is a class which, because of the ignorance in which it has been kept and the isolation in which it lives, requires the revolutionary and political leadership of the working class and the revolutionary intellectuals. Without that, it cannot alone launch the struggle and achieve victory.

In the present historical conditions of Latin America, the national bourgeoisie cannot lead the antifeudal and anti-imperialist struggle. Experience demonstrates that in our nations this class—even when its interests clash with those of Yankee imperialism—has been incapable of confronting imperialism, paralyzed by fear of social revolution and frightened by the clamor of the exploited masses.

Completing the foresight of the preceding statements, which constitute the essence of the revolutionary declaration of Latin America, the Second Declaration of Havana in the following paragraphs states:

The subjective conditions in each country, the factors of revolutionary consciousness, of organization, of leadership, can accelerate or delay revolution, depending on the state of their development. Sooner or later, in each historic epoch, as objective conditions ripen, consciousness is acquired, organization is achieved, leadership arises, and revolution is produced.

Whether this takes place peacefully or comes into the world after painful labor does not depend on the revolutionaries; it depends on the reactionary forces of the old society. Revolution, in history, is like the doctor who assists at the birth of a new life: he does not use forceps unless necessary, but he will unhesitatingly use them every time labor requires them. It is a labor which brings the hope of a better life to the enslaved and exploited masses.

In many Latin American countries revolution is inevitable. This fact is not determined by the will of anyone. It is determined by the horrible conditions of exploitation under which the American people live, the development of a revolutionary consciousness in the masses, the worldwide crisis of imperialism, and the universal liberation movements of the subjugated nations.

We shall begin from this basis to analyze the whole matter of guerrilla warfare in Latin America.

We have already established that it is a means of struggle to attain an end. First, our concern is to analyze the end in order to determine whether the winning of power in Latin America can be achieved in other ways than armed struggle. Peaceful struggle can be carried out through mass movements compelling—in special crisis situations—the governments to yield; thus, eventually the popular forces would take over and establish a dictatorship of the proletariat. Theoretically this is correct. When analyzing this in the Latin American context, we must reach the following conclusions: Generally on this continent there exist objective conditions which propel the masses to violent actions against their bourgeois and landlord governments. In many countries there exist crises of power and also some subjective conditions for revolution. It is clear, of course, that in those countries where all of these conditions are found, it would be criminal not to act to seize power. In other countries where these conditions do not occur, it is right that different alternatives will appear and out of theoretical discussions the tactic proper to each country should emerge. The only thing which history does not admit is that the analysts and executors of proletarian policy be mistaken.

No one can solicit the role of vanguard of the party as if it were a diploma given by a university. To be the vanguard of the party means to be at the forefront of the working class through the struggle for achieving power. It means to know how to guide this fight through shortcuts to victory. This is the mission of our revolutionary parties and thus the analysis must be profound and exhaustive so that there will be no mistakes.

At the present time we can observe in America an unstable balance between oligarchical dictatorship and popular pressure. We mean by "oligarchical" the reactionary alliance between the bourgeoisie and the landowning class of each country which has a greater or lesser preponderance of feudalism.

These dictatorships carry on within a certain "legal" framework which they adjudicated themselves to facilitate their work throughout the unrestricted period of their class domination. Yet we are passing through a stage in which the masses' pressure is very strong and is straining bourgeois legality so that its own authors must violate it in order to halt the impetus of the masses.

Barefaced violation of all legislation or of laws specifically instituted to sanction ruling class deeds only increases the tension of the people's forces. Thus the oligarchical dictatorship attempts to use the old legal order to change constitutionality and further oppress the proletariat without a frontal clash. Nevertheless, at this point, a contradiction arises. The people no longer support the old much less the new coercive measures established by the dictatorship and try to smash them. We should never forget the class character, authoritarian and restrictive, which typifies the bourgeois state. Lenin refers to it in the following manner: "The state is the product and the manifestation of the irreconcilability of class antagonisms. The state arises when, where, and to the extent that class antagonisms objectively cannot be reconciled. And, conversely, the existence of the state proves that class antagonisms are irreconcilable." (*State and Revolution*)

In other words, we should not allow the word "democracy" to be utilized apologetically to represent the dictatorship of the exploiting classes and to lose its deeper meaning and acquire the meaning of granting the people certain liberties, more or less good. To struggle only to restore a certain degree of bourgeois legality without considering the question of revolutionary power is to struggle for the return of a dictatorial order established by the dominant social classes. In other words, it is to struggle for a lighter iron ball to be fixed to the prisoner's chain.

In these conditions of conflict, the oligarchy breaks its own contracts, its own mask of "democracy," and attacks the people, though it will always try to use the superstructure it has formed for oppression. Thus, we are faced once again with a dilemma: What must be done? Our reply is: Violence is not the monopoly of the exploiters and as such the exploited can use it too and, what is more, ought to use it when the moment arrives. Martí said, "He who wages war in a country, when he can avoid it, is a criminal, just as he who fails to promote war which cannot be avoided is a criminal."

Lenin said, "Social democracy has never taken a sentimental view of war. It unreservedly condemns war as a bestial means of settling conflicts in human society. But social democracy knows that as long as society is divided into classes, as long as there is exploitation of man by man, wars are inevitable. In order to end this exploitation we cannot walk away from war, which is always and everywhere begun by the exploiters, by the ruling and oppressing classes." He said this in 1905. Later in the "Military Program of the Proletarian Revolution," a far-reaching analysis of the nature of class struggle, he affirmed: "Whoever recognizes the class struggle cannot fail to recognize civil wars, which in every class society are the natural, and under certain conditions, inevitable continuation, development, and intensification of the class struggle. All the great revolutions prove this. To repudiate civil war, or to forget about it, would mean sinking into extreme opportunism and renouncing the socialist revolution." That is to say, we should not fear violence, the midwife of new societies; but violence should be unleashed at that precise moment in which the leaders have found the most favorable circumstances.

What will these be? Subjectively, they depend on two factors which complement each other and which deepen during the struggle: consciousness of the necessity of change and confidence in the possibility of this revolutionary change. Both of these factors, with the objective conditions (which are favorable in all Latin America for the development of the struggle), with the firm will to achieve it as well as the new correlation of forces in the world, will determine the mode of action.

Regardless of how far away the socialist countries may be, their favorable influence will be felt by the people who struggle, just as their example will give the people further strength. Fidel Castro said on July 26 [1963]: "And the duty of the revolutionaries, especially at this moment, is to know how to recognize and how to take advantage of the changes in the correlation of forces which have taken place in the world and to understand that these changes facilitate the people's struggle. The duty of revolutionaries, of Latin American revolutionaries, is not to wait for the change in the correlation of forces to produce a miracle of social revolutions in Latin America but to take full advantage of everything in it that is favorable to the revolutionary movement—and to make revolution!"

There are some who say, "Let us admit that in certain specific cases revolutionary war is the best means to achieve political power; but where do we find the great leaders, the Fidel Castros, who will lead us to victory?" Fidel Castro, as any human being, is the product of history. The political and military chieftains who will lead the insurrectional uprisings in America, merged if possible in one man, will learn the art of war during the course of war itself. There is neither trade nor profession that can be learned from books alone. In this case, the struggle itself is the great teacher.

Of course, the task will not be easy nor is it exempt from grave dangers throughout. During the development of armed struggle, there are two moments of extreme danger for the future of the revolution. The first of these arises in the preparatory stage and the way with which it is dealt will give the measure of determination to struggle as well as clarity of purpose of the people's forces. When the bourgeois state advances against the people's positions, obviously there must arise a process of defense against the enemy who at this point, being superior, attacks. If the basic subjective and objective conditions are ripe, the defense must be armed so that the popular forces will not merely become recipients of the enemy's blows. Nor should the armed defense camp be allowed to be transformed into the refuge of the pursued.

Guerrilla warfare may adopt a defensive movement at a certain point, yet it carries within itself the capacity to attack the enemy and must develop it constantly. This capacity is what determines, with the passing of time, the catalytic character of the people's forces. That is, guerrilla warfare is not passive self-defense; it is defense with attack. And from the moment we recognize it as such, it has as its final goal the conquest of political power.

This moment is important. In social processes the difference between violence and nonviolence cannot be measured by the number of shots exchanged; rather, it lies in concrete and fluctuating situations. And we must be able to see the right moment in which the people's forces, conscious of their relative weakness and their strategic strength, must take the initiative against the enemy so the situation will not deteriorate. The equilibrium between oligarchic dictatorship and the popular pressure must be changed. The dictatorship tries to function without resorting to force. Thus, we must try to oblige the dictatorship to resort to violence, thereby unmasking its true nature as the dictatorship of the reactionary social classes. This event will deepen the struggle to such an extent that there will be no retreat from it. The performance of the people's forces depends on the task of forcing the dictatorship to a decision—to retreat or unleash the struggle—thus beginning the stage of long-range armed action.

The skillful avoidance of the next dangerous moment depends on the growing power of the people's forces. Marx always recommended that once the revolutionary process has begun the proletariat strike blows again and again without rest. A revolution which does not constantly expand is a revolution which regresses. The fighters, if weary, begin to lose faith; and at this point some of the bourgeois maneuvers may bear fruit—for example, the holding of elections to turn the government to another gentleman with a sweeter voice and more angelic face than the outgoing tyrant or the staging of a coup by reactionaries generally led by the army with the direct or indirect support of the progressive forces. There are others, but it is not our intention to analyze such tactical stratagems.

Let us emphasize the military coup mentioned previously. What can the military contribute to democracy? What kind of loyalty can be asked of them if they are merely an instrument for the domination of the reactionary classes and imperialist monopolies and if, as a caste whose worth rests on the weapon in their hands, they aspire only to maintain their prerogatives?

When, in difficult situations for the oppressors, the military establishment conspires to overthrow a dictator who in fact has been defeated, it can be said that they do so because the dictator is unable to preserve their class prerogatives without extreme violence, a method which generally does not suit the interests of the oligarchies at that point.

This statement does not mean to reject the service of military men as individual fighters who, once separated from the society they served, have in fact now rebelled against it. They should be used in accordance with the revolutionary line they adopt as fighters and not as representatives of a caste.

A long time ago Engels, in the preface to the third edition of *Civil War in France,* wrote,

> The workers were armed after every revolution; for this reason the disarming of the workers was the first commandment for the bourgeois at the helm of the state. Hence, after every revolution won by the workers, a new struggle ending with the defeat of the workers. (Quoted by Lenin in *State and Revolution*)

This play of continuous struggle, in which some change is obtained and then strategically withdrawn, has been repeated for many dozens of years in the capitalist world. Moreover, the permanent deception of the proletariat along these lines has been practiced for over a century.

There is danger also that progressive party leaders, wishing to maintain conditions more favorable for revolutionary action through the use of certain aspects of bourgeois legality, will lose sight of their goal (which is common during the action), thus forgetting the primary strategic objective: the seizure of power.

These two difficult moments in the revolution, which we have analyzed briefly, become obvious when the leaders of

Marxist-Leninist parties are capable of perceiving the implications of the moment clearly and of mobilizing the masses to the fullest, leading them on the correct path of resolving fundamental contradictions.

In developing the thesis, we have assumed that eventually the idea of armed struggle as well as the formula of guerrilla warfare as a method of struggle will be accepted. Why do we think that in the present situation of America guerrilla warfare is the best method? There are fundamental arguments which in our opinion determine the necessity of guerrilla action as the central axis of struggle in Latin America.

First, accepting as true that the enemy will fight to maintain itself in power, one must think about destroying the oppressor army. To do this, a people's army is necessary. This army is not born spontaneously; rather it must be armed from the enemy's arsenal and this requires a long and difficult struggle in which the people's forces and their leaders will always be exposed to attack from superior forces and be without adequate conditions of defense and maneuverability.

On the other hand, the guerrilla nucleus, established in terrain favorable for the struggle, ensures the security and continuity of the revolutionary command. The urban forces, led by the general staff of the people's army, can perform actions of the greatest importance. However, the eventual destruction of these groups would not kill the soul of the revolution; its leadership would continue from its rural bastion to spark the revolutionary spirit of the masses and would continue to organize new forces for other battles.

Moreover, in this region begins the construction of the future state apparatus entrusted to lead the class dictatorship efficiently during the transition period. The longer the struggle becomes, the larger and more complex the administrative problems; and in solving them, cadres will be trained for the difficult task of consolidating power and, at a later stage, economic development.

Second, there is the general situation of the Latin American peasantry and the ever more explosive character of the struggle against feudal structures within the framework of an alliance between local and foreign exploiters.

Returning to the Second Declaration of Havana,

At the outset of the past century, the peoples of America freed themselves from Spanish colonialism, but they did not free themselves from exploitation. The feudal landlords assumed the authority of the governing Spaniards, the Indians continued in their painful serfdom, the Latin American man remained a slave one way or another, and the minimum hopes of the peoples died under the power of the oligarchies and the tyranny of foreign capital. This is the truth of America, to one or another degree of variation. Latin America today is under a more ferocious imperialism, more powerful and ruthless, than the Spanish colonial empire.

What is Yankee imperialism's attitude confronting the objective and historically inexorable reality of the Latin American revolution? To prepare to fight a colonial war against the peoples of Latin America; to create an apparatus of force to establish the political pretexts and the pseudo-legal instruments underwritten by the representatives of the reactionary oligarchies in order to curb, by blood and by iron, the struggle of the Latin American peoples.

This objective situation shows the dormant force of our peasants and the need to utilize it for Latin America's liberation.

Third, there is the continental nature of the struggle. Could we imagine this stage of Latin American emancipation as the confrontation of two local forces struggling for power in a specific territory? Hardly. The struggle between the people's forces and the forces of repression will be to the death. This too is predicted by the paragraphs cited previously.

The Yankees will intervene due to solidarity of interest and because the struggle in Latin America is decisive. As a matter of fact, they are intervening already as they prepare the forces of repression and the organization of a continental apparatus of struggle. But, from now on, they will do so with all their energies; they will punish the popular forces with all the destructive weapons at their disposal. They will not allow a revolutionary power to consolidate; and, if it ever happens, they will attack again, will not recognize it, and will try to divide the revolutionary forces. Moreover, they will infiltrate saboteurs, create border problems, will force other reactionary states to oppose it, and will impose economic sanctions attempting, in one word, to annihilate the new state.

This being the panorama in Latin America, it is difficult to achieve and consolidate victory in a country which is isolated. The unity of the repressive forces must be confronted with the unity of the popular forces. In all countries where oppression reaches intolerable proportions, the banner of rebellion must be raised; and this banner of historical necessity will have a continental character.

As Fidel stated, the cordilleras of the Andes will be the Sierra Maestra of Latin America; and the immense territories which this continent encompasses will become the scene of a life or death struggle against imperialism.

We cannot predict when this struggle will reach a continental dimension nor how long it will last. But we can predict its advent and triumph because it is the inevitable result of historical, economic, and political conditions; and its direction cannot change.

The task of the revolutionary forces in each country is to initiate the struggle when the conditions are present there, regardless of the conditions in other countries. The development of the struggle will bring about the general strategy. The prediction of the continental character of the struggle is the outcome of the analysis of the strength of each contender, but this does not exclude independent outbreaks. As the beginning of the struggle in one area of a country is bound to cause its development throughout the region, the beginning of a revolutionary war contributes to the development of new conditions in the neighboring countries.

The development of revolution has normally produced high and low tides in inverse proportion. To the revolution's high tide corresponds the counterrevolutionary low tide and vice versa, as there is a counterrevolutionary ascendancy at moments of revolutionary decline. In those moments, the situation of the people's forces becomes difficult; and they should resort to the best means of defense in order to suffer the least damage. The enemy is extremely powerful, it is of continental scope. For this reason, the relative weakness of the local bourgeoisie cannot be analyzed with a view toward making decisions within restricted boundaries. Still less can one think of an eventual alliance by these oligarchies with a people in arms.

The Cuban Revolution sounded the bell which gave the alarm. The polarization of forces will become complete: exploiters on one side and exploited on the other. And the mass of the petty bourgeoisie will lean to one side or the other according to their interests and the political skill with which they are handled. Thus, neutrality will be an exception. This is how revolutionary war will be.

Let us think how a guerrilla focus can start. Nuclei with relatively few persons choose places favorable for guerrilla warfare, with the intention of unleashing a counterattack or to weather the storm, and there they start taking action. However, what follows must be very clear: At the beginning the relative weakness of the guerrilla is such that they should work only toward becoming acquainted with the terrain and its surroundings while establishing connections with the population and fortifying the places which eventually will be converted into bases.

A guerrilla force which has just begun its development must follow three conditions in order to survive: constant mobility, constant vigilance, constant distrust. Without the adequate use of these three conditions of military tactics, the guerrilla will find it hard to survive. We must remember that the heroism of the guerrilla fighter, at this moment, consists of the scope of the planned goal and the enormous number of sacrifices that he must make in order to achieve it. These sacrifices are not made in daily combat or face-to-face battle with the enemy; rather, they will adopt more subtle and difficult forms for the guerrilla fighter to resist physically and mentally.

Perhaps the guerrillas will be punished heavily by the enemy, divided at times into groups with those who are captured to be tortured. They will be pursued as hunted animals in areas where they have chosen to operate; the constant anxiety of having the enemy on their track will be with them. They must distrust everyone, for the terrorized peasants in some cases will give them away to the repressive troops in order to save themselves. Their only alternatives are life or death, at times when death is a concept a thousand times present and victory only a myth for a revolutionary to dream of.

This is the guerrilla's heroism. This is why it is said that walking is a form of fighting and to avoid combat at a given moment is also another form. Facing the general superiority of the enemy at a given place, one must find a form of tactics with which to gain a relative superiority at that moment either by being capable of concentrating more troops than the enemy or by using fully and well the terrain in order to secure advantages that unbalance the correlation of forces. In these conditions, tactical victory is assured; if relative superiority is not clear, it is better not to act. As long as the guerrilla is in the position of deciding the "how" and the "when," no combat should be fought that will not end in victory.

Within the framework of the great politicomilitary action, of which they are a part, the guerrilla will grow and reach consolidation. Thus, bases will continue to be formed, for they are essential to the success of the guerrilla army. These bases are points which the enemy can enter only at the cost of heavy losses; they are the revolution's bastions, both refuge and starting point for the guerrilla's more daring and distant raids.

One comes to this point if difficulties of a tactical and political nature have been overcome. The guerrillas cannot forget their function as vanguard of the people—their mandate—and as such they must create the necessary political conditions for the establishment of a revolutionary power based on the masses' support. The peasants' aspirations or demands must be satisfied to the degree and form which circumstances permit so as to bring about the decisive support and solidarity of the whole population.

If the military situation will be difficult from the very first moment, the political situation will be just as delicate; if a single military error can liquidate the guerrilla, a political error can hold back its development for long periods. The struggle is politico-military and as such it must be developed and understood.

In the process of the guerrilla growth, the fighting reaches a point where its capacity for action covers a given region for which there are too many men in too great a concentration in the area. There begins the beehive action in which one of the commanders, a distinguished guerrilla, hops to another region and repeats the chain of development of guerrilla warfare. He is, nevertheless, subject to a central command.

It is imperative to point out that one cannot hope for victory without the formation of a popular army. The guerrilla forces can be expanded to a certain magnitude; the people's forces, in the cities and in other areas, can inflict losses; but the military potential of the reactionaries will still remain intact. One must always keep in mind the fact that the final objective is the enemy's annihilation. Therefore, all these new zones which are being created, as well as the zones infiltrated behind enemy lines and the forces operating in the principal cities, should be under one unified command.

Guerrilla war or war of liberation will generally have three stages: First, the strategic defensive when the small force nibbles at the enemy and runs; it is not sheltered to make a passive defense within a small circumference but rather its defense consists of the limited attacks which it can strike successfully. After this comes a state of equilibrium in which the possibilities of action on both sides—the enemy and the guerrillas—are established. Finally, the last stage consists of overrunning the repressive army leading to the capture of the big cities, large-scale decisive encounters, and at last the complete annihilation of the enemy.

After reaching a state of equilibrium when both sides respect each other and as the war's development continues, the guerrilla war acquires new characteristics. The concept of maneuver is introduced: large columns which attack strong points; mobile warfare with the shifting of forces and means of attack of relative potential. But due to the capacity for resistance and counterattack that the enemy still has, this war of maneuver does not replace guerrilla fighting: rather, it is only one form of action taken by the guerrillas until that time when they crystallize into a people's army with an army corps. Even at this moment the guerrilla, marching ahead of the action of the main forces, will play the role of its first stage, destroying communications and sabotaging the whole defensive apparatus of the enemy.

We have predicted that the war will be continental. This means that it will be a protracted war; it will have many fronts; and it will cost much blood and countless lives for a long period of time. But another phenomenon occurring in Latin America is the polarization of forces, that is, the clear division between exploiters and exploited. Thus when the armed vanguard of the people achieves power, both the imperialists and the national exploiting class will be liquidated at one stroke. The first stage of the socialist revolution will have crystallized, and the people will be ready to heal their wounds and initiate the construction of socialism.

Are there possibilities less bloody? Awhile ago the last dividing up of the world took place in which the United States took the lion's share of our continent. Today the imperialists of the Old World are developing again—and the strength of the European Common Market frightens the United States itself. All this might lead to the belief that there exists the possibility for us merely to observe as spectators the struggle among the imperialists trying to make further advances, perhaps in alliance with the stronger national bourgeoisie. Yet a passive policy never brings good results in class struggle and alliances with the bourgeoisie, though they might appear to be revolutionary, have only a transitory character. The time factor will induce us to choose another ally. The sharpening of the most important contradiction in Latin America appears to be so rapid that it disturbs the "normal" development of the imperialist camp's contradiction in its struggle for markets.

The majority of national bourgeoisie have united with North American imperialism; thus their fate shall be the same as that of the latter. Even in the cases where pacts or common contradictions are shared between the national bourgeoisie and other imperialists, this occurs within the framework of a fundamental struggle which will embrace sooner or later *all the exploited and all the exploiters.* The polarization of antagonistic forces among class adversaries is up till now more rapid than the development of the contradiction among exploiters over the splitting of the spoils. There are two camps: the alternative becomes clearer for each individual and for each specific stratum of the population.

The Alliance for Progress attempts to slow that which cannot be stopped. But if the advance of the European Common Market or any other imperialist group on the American market were more rapid than the development of the fundamental contradiction, the forces of the people would only have to penetrate into the open breach, carrying on the struggle and using the new intruders with a clear awareness of what their true intentions are.

Not a single position, weapon, or secret should be given to the class enemy, under penalty of losing all. In fact, the eruption of the Latin American struggle has begun. Will its storm center be in Venezuela, Guatemala, Colombia, Peru, Ecuador? Are today's skirmishes only manifestations of a restlessness that has not come to fruition? The outcome of today's struggles does not matter. It does not matter in the final count that one or two movements were temporarily defeated because what is definite is the decision to struggle which matures every day, the consciousness of the need for revolutionary change, and the certainty that it is possible.

This is a prediction. We make it with the conviction that history will prove us right. The analysis of the objective and subjective conditions of Latin America and the imperialist world indicates to us the certainty of these assertions based on the Second Declaration of Havana.

SOURCE: *Cuba Socialista* (Havana), September 1963, pp. 1–17.

MESSAGE TO THE TRICONTINENTAL (1967)

MESSAGE TO THE TRICONTINENTAL

Now is the time of the furnaces, and
only light should be seen.

José Martí

Twenty-one years have already elapsed since the end of the last world conflagration; numerous publications, in every possible language, celebrate this event, symbolized by the defeat of Japan. There is a climate of apparent optimism in many areas of the different camps into which the world is divided.

Twenty-one years without a world war, in these times of maximum confrontations, of violent clashes and sudden changes, appears to be a very high figure. However, without analyzing the practical results of this peace (poverty, degradation, increasingly larger exploitation of enormous sectors of humanity) for which all of us have stated that we are willing to fight, we would do well to inquire if this peace is real.

It is not the purpose of these notes to detail the different conflicts of a local character that have been occurring since the surrender of Japan, neither do we intend to recount the numerous and increasing instances of civilian strife which have taken place during these years of apparent peace. It will be enough just to name, as an example against undue optimism, the wars of Korea and Vietnam.

In the first one, after years of savage warfare, the Northern part of the country was submerged in the most terrible devastation known in the annals of modern warfare: riddled with bombs; without factories, schools or hospitals; with absolutely no shelter for housing ten million inhabitants.

Under the discredited flag of the United Nations, dozens of countries under the military leadership of the United States participated in this war with the massive intervention of U.S. soldiers and the use, as cannon fodder, of the South Korean population that was enrolled. On the other side, the army and the people of Korea and the volunteers from the Peoples' Republic of China were furnished with supplies and advice by the Soviet military apparatus. The U.S. tested all sorts of weapons of destruction, excluding the thermonuclear type, but including, on a limited scale, bacteriological and chemical warfare.

In Vietnam, the patriotic forces of that country have carried on an almost uninterrupted war against three imperialist powers: Japan, whose might suffered an almost vertical collapse after the bombs of Hiroshima and Nagasaki; France, who recovered from that defeated country its Indo-China colonies and ignored the promises it had made in harder times; and the United States, in this last phase of the struggle.

There were limited confrontations in every continent although in Our America, for a long time, there were only incipient liberation struggles and military coups d'etat until the Cuban revolution resounded the alert, signaling the importance of this region. This action attracted the wrath of the imperialists and Cuba was finally obliged to defend its coasts, first in Playa Girón, and again during the Missile Crisis.

This last incident could have unleashed a war of incalculable proportions if a U.S.-Soviet clash had occurred over the Cuban question.

But, evidently, the focal point of all contradictions is at present the territory of the peninsula of Indo-China and the adjacent areas. Laos and Vietnam are torn by a civil war which has ceased being such by the entry into the conflict of U.S. imperialism with all its might, thus transforming the whole zone into a dangerous detonator ready at any moment to explode.

In Vietnam the confrontation has assumed extremely acute characteristics. It is not our intention, either, to chronicle this war. We shall simply remember and point out some milestones.

In 1954, after the annihilating defeat of Dien-Bien-Phu, an agreement was signed at Geneva dividing the country into two separate zones; elections were to be held within a term of 18 months to determine who should govern Vietnam and how the country should be reunified. The U.S. did not sign this document and started maneuvering to substitute the emperor, Bao-Dai, who was a French puppet, for a man more amiable to its purposes. This happened to be Ngo-Din-Diem, whose tragic end—that of an orange squeezed dry by imperialism—is well known by all.

During the months following the agreement, optimism reigned supreme in the camp of the popular forces. The last pockets of the anti-French resistance were dismantled in the South of the country—and they awaited the fulfillment of the Geneva agreements. But the patriots soon realized there would be no elections—unless the United States felt itself capable of imposing its will in the polls, which was practically impossible even resorting to all its fraudulent methods. Once again the fighting broke out in the South and gradually acquired full intensity. At present the U.S. army has increased to over half a million invaders while the puppet forces decrease in number and, above all, have totally lost their combativeness.

Almost two years ago the United States started bombing systematically the Democratic Republic of Vietnam, in yet another attempt to overcome the belligerance [*sic*] of the South and impose, from a position of strength, a meeting at the conference table. At first, the bombardments were more or less isolated occurrences and were adorned with the mask of reprisals for alleged provocations from the North. Later on, as they increased in intensity and regularity, they became one gigantic attack carried out by the air force of the United States, day after day, for the purpose of destroying all vestiges of civilization in the Northern zone of the country. This is an episode of the infamously notorious "escalation."

The material aspirations of the Yankee world have been fulfilled to a great extent, regardless of the unflinching defense of the Vietnamese anti-aircraft artillery, of the numerous planes shot down (over 1,700) and of the socialist countries aid in war supplies.

There is a sad reality: Vietnam—a nation representing the

aspirations, the hopes of a whole world of forgotten peoples—is tragically alone. This nation must endure the furious attacks of U.S. technology, with practically no possibility of reprisals in the South and only some of defense in the North—but always alone.

The solidarity of all progressive forces of the world towards the people of Vietnam today is similar to the bitter irony of the plebeians coaxing on the gladiators in the Roman arena. It is not a matter of wishing success to the victim of aggression, but of sharing his fate; one must accompany him to his death or to victory.

When we analyze the lonely situation of the Vietnamese people, we are overcome by anguish at this illogical moment of humanity.

U.S. imperialism is guilty of aggression—its crimes are enormous and cover the whole world. We already know all that, gentlemen! But this guilt also applies to those who, when the time came for a definition, hesitated to make Vietnam an inviolable part of the socialist world; running, of course, the risks of a war on a global scale—but also forcing a decision upon imperialism. And the guilt also applies to those who maintain a war of abuse and snares—started quite some time ago by the representatives of the two greatest powers of the socialist camp.

We must ask ourselves, seeking an honest answer: Is Vietnam isolated, or is it not? Is it not maintaining a dangerous equilibrium between the two quarrelling powers?

And what great people these are! What stoicism and courage! And what a lesson for the world is contained in this struggle! Not for a long time shall we be able to know if President Johnson ever seriously thought of bringing about some of the reforms needed by his people—to iron out the barbed class contradictions that grow each day with explosive power. The truth is that the improvements announced under the pompous title of the "Great Society" have dropped into the cesspool of Vietnam.

The largest of all imperialist powers feels in its own guts the bleeding inflicted by a poor and underdeveloped country; its fabulous economy feels the strain of the war effort. Murder is ceasing to be the most convenient business for its monopolies.

Defensive weapons, and never in adequate number, is all these extraordinary soldiers have—besides love for their homeland, their society, and unsurpassed courage. But imperialism is bogging down in Vietnam, is unable to find a way out and desperately seeks one that will overcome with dignity this dangerous situation in which it now finds itself. Furthermore, the Four Points put forward by the North and the Five Points of the South now corner imperialism, making the confrontation even more decisive.

Everything indicate [*sic*] that peace, this unstable peace which bears that name for the sole reason that no worldwide conflagration has taken place, is again in danger of being destroyed by some irrevocable and unacceptable step taken by the United States.

What role shall we, the exploited people of the world, play? The peoples of the three continents focus their attention on Vietnam and learn their lesson. Since imperialists blackmail humanity by threatening it with war, the wise reaction is not to fear war. The general tactics of the people should be to launch a constant and a firm attack in all fronts where the confrontation is taking place.

In those places where this meager peace we have has been violated, which is our duty? To liberate ourselves at any price.

The world panorama is of great complexity. The struggle for liberation has not yet been undertaken by some countries of ancient Europe, sufficiently developed to realize the contradictions of capitalism, but weak to such a degree that they are unable either to follow imperialism or even to start on its own road. Their contradictions will reach an explosive stage during the forthcoming years—but their problems and, consequently, their own solutions are different from those of our dependent and economically underdeveloped countries.

The fundamental field of imperialist exploitation comprises the three underdeveloped continents: America, Asia, and Africa. Every country has also its own characteristics, but each continent, as a whole, also presents a certain unity.

Our America is integrated by a group of more or less homogeneous countries and in most parts of its territory U.S. monopolist capitals maintain an absolute supremacy. Puppet governments or, in the best of cases, weak and fearful local rulers, are incapable of contradicting orders from their Yankee master. The United States has nearly reached the climax of its political and economic domination; it could hardly advance much more; any change in the situation could bring about a setback. Their policy is to maintain that which has already been conquered. The line of action, at the present time, is limited to the brutal use of force with the purpose of thwarting the liberation movements, no matter of what type they might happen to be.

The slogan "we will not allow another Cuba" hides the possibility of perpetrating aggressions without fear of reprisal, such as the one carried out against the Dominican Republic or before that the massacre in Panama—and the clear warning stating that Yankee troops are ready to intervene anywhere in America where the ruling regime may be altered, thus endangering their interests. This policy enjoys an almost absolute impunity: the OAS is a suitable mask, in spite of its unpopularity; the inefficiency of the UN is ridiculous as well as tragic; the armies of all American countries are ready to intervene in order to smash their peoples. The International of Crime and Treason [*sic*] has in fact been organized. On the other hand, the autochthonous bourgeoisies have lost all their capacity to oppose imperialism—if they ever had it—and they have become the last card in the pack. There are no other alternatives; either a socialist revolution or a make-believe revolution.

Asia is a continent with many different characteristics. The struggle for liberation waged against a series of European colonial powers resulted in the establishment of more or less progressive governments, whose ulterior evolution have brought about, in some cases, the deepening of the primary objectives of national liberation and in others, a setback towards the adoption of pro-imperialist positions.

From the economic point of view, the United States had very little to lose and much to gain from Asia. These changes benefited its interests; the struggle for the overthrow of other neocolonial powers and the penetration of new spheres of action in the economic field is carried out sometimes directly, occasionally through Japan.

But there are special political conditions, particularly in Indo-China, which create in Asia certain characteristics of capital importance and play a decisive role in the entire U.S. military strategy.

The imperialists encircle China through South Korea, Japan, Taiwan, South Vietnam and Thailand at least.

This dual situation, a strategic interest as important as the military encirclement of the Peoples' Republic of China and the penetration of these great markets—which they do not dominate yet—turns Asia into one of the most explosive points of the world today, in spite of its apparent stability outside of the Vietnamese war zone.

The Middle East, though it geographically belongs to this continent, has its own contradictions and is actively in ferment; it is impossible to foretell how far this cold war between Israel, backed by the imperialists, and the progressive countries of that zone will go. This is just another one of the volcanoes threatening eruption in the world today.

Africa offers an almost virgin territory to the neocolonial invasion. There have been changes which, to some extent, forced neocolonial powers to give up their former absolute prerogatives. But when these changes are carried out uninterruptedly, colonialism continues in the form of neocolonialism with similar effects as far as the economic situation is concerned.

The United States had no colonies in this region but is now struggling to penetrate its partners' fiefs. It can be said that following the strategic plans of U.S. imperialism, Africa constitutes its long range reservoir; its present investments, though, are only important in the Union of South Africa and its penetration is beginning to be felt in the Congo, Nigeria and other countries where a violent rivalry with other imperialist powers is beginning to take place (in a pacific manner up to the present time).

So far it does not have there great interests to defend except its pretended right to intervene in every spot of the world where its monopolies detect huge profits or the existence of large reserves of raw materials.

All this past history justifies our concern regarding the possibilities of liberating the peoples within a long or a short period of time.

If we stop to analyze Africa we shall observe that in the Portuguese colonies of Guinea, Mozambique and Angola the struggle is waged with relative intensity, with a concrete success in the first one and with variable success in the other two. We still witness in the Congo the dispute between Lumumba's successors and the old accomplices of Tshombe, a dispute which at the present time seems to favor the latter: those who have "pacified" a large area of the country for their own benefit—though the war is still latent.

In Rhodesia we have a different problem: British imperialism used every means within its reach to place power in the hands of the white minority, who, at the present time, unlawfully holds it. The conflict, from the British point of view, is absolutely unofficial; this Western power, with its habitual diplomatic cleverness—also called hypocrisy in the strict sense of the word—presents a facade of displeasure before the measures adopted by the government of Ian Smith. Its crafty attitude is supported by some Commonwealth countries that follow it, but is attacked by a large group of countries belonging to Black Africa, whether they are or not servile economic lackeys of British imperialism.

Should the rebellious efforts of these patriots succeed and this movement receive the effective support of neighboring African nations, the situation in Rhodesia may become extremely explosive. But for the moment all these problems are being discussed in harmless organizations such as the UN, the Commonwealth and the OAU.

The social and political evolution of Africa does not lead us to expect a continental revolution. The liberation struggle against the Portuguese should end victoriously, but Portugal does not mean anything in the imperialist field. The confrontations of revolutionary importance are those which place at bay all the imperialist apparatus; this does not mean, however, that we should stop fighting for the liberation of the three Portuguese colonies and for the deepening of their revolutions.

When the black masses of South Africa or Rhodesia start their authentic revolutionary struggle, a new era will dawn in Africa. Or when the impoverished masses of a nation rise up to rescue their right to a decent life from the hands of the ruling oligarchies.

Up to now, army putsches follow one another; a group of officers succeeds another or substitute a ruler who no longer serves their caste interests or those of the powers who covertly manage him—but there are no great popular upheavals. In the Congo these characteristics appeared briefly, generated by the memory of Lumumba, but they have been losing strength in the last few months.

In Asia, as we have seen, the situation is explosive. The points of friction are not only Vietnam and Laos, where there is fighting; such a point is also Cambodia, where at any time a direct U.S. aggression may start, Thailand, Malaya, and, of course, Indonesia, where we can not assume that the last word has been said, regardless of the annihilation of the Communist Party in that country when the reactionaries took over. And also, naturally, the Middle East.

In Latin America the armed struggle is going on in Guatemala, Colombia, Venezuela and Bolivia; the first uprisings are cropping up in Brazil [*sic*]. There are also some resistance focuses which appear and then are extinguished. But almost all the countries of this continent are ripe for a type of struggle that, in order to achieve victory, cannot be content with anything less than establishing a government of socialist tendencies.

In this continent practically only one tongue is spoken (with the exception of Brazil, with whose people, those who speak Spanish can easily make themselves understood, owing to the great similarity of both languages). There is also such a great similarity between the classes in these countries, that they have attained identification among themselves of an *internacional americano* type, much more complete than in the other continents. Language, habits, religion, a common foreign master, unite them. The degree and the form of exploitation are similar for both the exploiters and the men they exploit in the majority of the countries of Our America. And rebellion is ripening swiftly in it.

We may ask ourselves: how shall this rebellion flourish? What type will it be? We have maintained for quite some time now that, owing to the similarity of their characteristics, the struggle in Our America will achieve, in due course, continental proportions. It shall be the scene of many great battles fought for the liberation of humanity.

Within the frame of this struggle of continental scale, the battles which are now taking place are only episodes—but they have already furnished their martyrs, they shall figure in the history of Our America as having given their necessary blood in this last stage of the fight for the total freedom of man. These names will include Comandante Turcios Lima, padre Camilo Torres, Comandante Fabricio Ojeda, Comandantes Lobatón and Luis de la Puente Uceda, all outstanding figures in the revolutionary movements of Guatemala, Colombia, Venezuela and Peru.

But the active movement of the people creates its new leaders; César Montes and Yon Sosa raise up their flag in Guatemala; Fabio Vázquez and Marulanda in Colombia; Douglas Bravo in the Western part of the country and Américo Martín in El Bachiller, both directing their respective Venezuelan fronts.

New uprisings shall take place in these and other countries of Our America, as it has already happened in Bolivia, and they shall continue to grow in the midst of all the hardships inherent to this dangerous profession of being modern revolutionaries. Many shall perish, victims of their errors; others shall fall in the touch battle that approaches; new fighters and new leaders shall appear in the warmth of the revolutionary struggle. The people shall create their warriors and leaders in the selective framework of the war itself—and Yankee agents of repression shall increase. Today there are military aids in all the countries where armed struggle is growing; the Peruvian army apparently carried out a successful action against the revolutionaries in that country, an army also trained and advised by the Yankees. But if the focuses of war grow with sufficient political and military insight, they shall become practically invincible and shall force the Yankees to send reinforcements. In Peru itself many new figures, practically unknown, are now reorganizing the guerrilla. Little by little, the obsolete weapons, which are sufficient for the repression of small armed bands, will be exchanged for modern armaments and the U.S. military aids will be substituted by actual fighters until, at a given moment, they are forced to send increasingly greater number of regular troops to ensure the relative stability of a government whose national puppet army is disintegrating before the impetuous attacks of the guerrillas. It is the road of Vietnam; it is the road that should be followed by the people; it is the road that will be followed in Our America, with the advantage that the armed groups could create Coordinating Councils to embarrass the repressive forces of Yankee imperialism and accelerate the revolutionary triumph.

America, a forgotten continent in the last liberation struggles, is now beginning to make itself heard through the Tricontinental and, in the voice of the vanguard of its peoples, the Cuban Revolution, will today have a task of much greater relevance: creating a Second or a Third Vietnam, or the Second *and* Third Vietnam of the world.

We must bear in mind that imperialism is a world system, the last stage of capitalism—and it must be defeated in a world confrontation. The strategic end of this struggle should be the destruction of imperialism. Our share, the responsibility of the exploited and underdeveloped of the world is to eliminate the foundations of imperialism: our oppressed nations, from where they extract capitals, raw materials, technicians and cheap labor, and to which they export new capitals—instruments of domination—arms and all kinds of articles; thus submerging us in an absolute dependance [*sic*].

The fundamental element of this strategic end shall be the real liberation of all people, a liberation that will be brought about through armed struggle in most cases and which shall be, in our America, almost indefectibly, a Socialist Revolution.

While envisaging the destruction of imperialism, it is necessary to identify its head, which is no other than the United States of America.

We must carry out a general task with the tactical purpose of getting the enemy out of its natural environment, forcing him to fight in regions where his own life and habits will clash with the existing reality. We must not underrate our adversary; the U.S. soldier has technical capacity and is backed by weapons and resources of such magnitude that render him frightful. He lacks the essential ideologic motivation which his bitterest enemies of today—the Vietnamese soldiers—have in the highest degree. We will only be able to overcome that army by undermining their morale—and this is accomplished by defeating it and causing it repeated sufferings.

But this brief outline of victories carries within itself the immense sacrifice of the people, sacrifices that should be demanded beginning today, in plain daylight, and which perhaps may be less painful than those we would have to endure if we constantly avoided battle in an attempt to have others pull our chestnuts out of the fire.

It is probable, of course, that the last liberated country shall accomplish this without an armed struggle and the sufferings of a long and cruel war against the imperialists—this they might avoid. But perhaps it will be impossible to avoid this struggle or its effects in a global conflagration; the suffering would be the same, or perhaps even greater. We cannot foresee the future, but we should never give in to the defeatist temptation of being the vanguard of a nation which yearns for freedom, but abhors the struggle it entails and awaits its freedom as a crumb of victory.

It is absolutely just to avoid all useless sacrifices. Therefore, it is so important to clear up the real possibilities that dependent America may have of liberating itself through pacific means. For us, the solution to this question is quite clear: the present moment may or may not be the proper one for starting the struggle, but we cannot harbor any illusions, and we have no right to do so, that freedom can be obtained without fighting. And these battles shall not be mere street fights with stones against tear-gas bombs, or of pacific general strikes; neither shall it be the battle of a furious people destroying in two or three days the repressive scaffolds of the ruling oligarchies; the struggle shall be long, harsh, and its front shall be in the guerrilla's refuge, in the cities, in the homes of the fighters—where the repressive forces shall go seeking easy victims among their families—in the massacred rural population, in the villages or cities destroyed by the bombardments of the enemy.

They are pushing us into this struggle; there is no alternative: we must prepare it and we must decide to undertake it.

The beginnings will not be easy; they shall be extremely difficult. All the oligarchies' powers of repression, all their capacity for brutality and demagoguery will be placed at the service of their cause. Our mission, in the first hour, shall be to survive;

later, we shall follow the perennial example of the guerrilla, carrying out armed propaganda (in the Vietnamese sense, that is, the bullets of propaganda, of the battles won or lost—but fought—against the enemy). The great lesson of the invincibility of the guerrillas taking root in the dispossessed masses. The galvanizing of the national spirit, the preparation for harder tasks, for resisting even more violent repressions. Hatred as an element of the struggle; a relentless hatred of the enemy, impelling us over and beyond the natural limitations that man is heir to and transforming him into an effective, violent, selective and cold killing machine. Our soldiers must be thus; a people without hatred cannot vanquish a brutal enemy.

We must carry the war into every corner the enemy happens to carry it: to his home, to his centers of entertainment; a total war. It is necessary to prevent him from having a moment of peace, a quiet moment outside his barracks or even inside; we must attack him wherever he may be; make him feel like a cornered beast wherever he may move. Then his moral fiber shall begin to decline. He will even become more beastly, but we shall notice how the signs of decadence begin to appear.

And let us develop a true proletarian internationalism; with international proletarian armies; the flag under which we fight would be the sacred cause of redeeming humanity. To die under the flag of Vietnam, of Venezuela, of Guatemala, of Laos, of Guinea, of Colombia, of Bolivia, of Brazil—to name only a few scenes of today's armed struggle—would be equally glorious and desirable for an American, an Asian, an African, even a European.

Each spilt drop of blood, in any country under whose flag one has not been born, is an experience passed on to those who survive, to be added later to the liberation struggle of his own country. And each nation liberated is a phase won in the battle for the liberation of one's own country.

The time has come to settle our discrepancies and place everything at the service of our struggle.

We all know great controversies rend the world now fighting for freedom; no one can hide it. We also know that they have reached such intensity and such bitterness that the possibility of dialogue and reconciliation seems extremely difficult, if not impossible. It is a useless task to search for means and ways to propitiate a dialogue which the hostile parties avoid. However, the enemy is there; it strikes every day, and threatens us with new blows and these blows will unite us, today, tomorrow, or the day after. Whoever understands this first, and prepares for this necessary union, shall have the people's gratitude.

Owing to the virulence and the intransigence with which each cause is defended, we, the dispossessed, cannot take sides for one form or the other of these discrepancies, even though sometimes we coincide with the contentions of one party or the other, or in a greater measure with those of one part more than with those of the other. In time of war, the expression of current differences constitutes a weakness; but at this stage it is an illusion to attempt to settle them by means of words. History shall erode them or shall give them their true meaning.

In our struggling world every discrepancy regarding tactics, the methods of action for the attainment of limited objectives should be analyzed with due respect to another man's opinions. Regarding our great strategic objective, the total destruction of imperialism by armed struggle, we should be uncompromising.

Let us sum up our hopes for victory: total destruction of imperialism by eliminating its firmest bulwark: the oppression exercised by the United States of America. To carry out, as a tactical method, the peoples' gradual liberation, one by one or in groups: driving the enemy into a difficult fight away from its own territory; dismantling all its sustenance bases, that is, its dependent territories.

This means a long war. And, once more we repeat it, a cruel war. Let no one fool himself at the outstart and let no one hesitate to start out for fear of the consequences it may bring to his people. It is almost our sole hope for victory. We cannot elude the call of this hour. Vietnam is pointing it out with its endless lesson of heroism, its tragic and everyday lesson of struggle and death for the attainment of final victory.

There, the imperialist soldiers endure the discomforts [*sic*] of those who, used to enjoying the U.S. standard of living, have to live in a hostile land with the insecurity of being unable to move without being aware of walking on enemy territory:—death to those who dare take a step out of their fortified encampment. The permanent hostility of the entire population. All this has internal repercussion in the United States; propitiates the resurgence of an element which is being minimized in spite of its vigor by all imperialist forces: class struggle even within its own territory.

How close we could look into a bright future should two, three or many Vietnams flourish throughout the world with their share of deaths and their immense tragedies, their everyday heroism and their repeated blows against imperialism, impelled to disperse its forces under the sudden attack and the increasing hatred of all peoples of the world!

And if we were all capable of uniting to make our blows stronger and infallible and so increase the effectiveness of all kinds of support given to the struggling people—how great and close would that future be!

If we, in a small point of the world map, are able to fulfill our duty and place at the disposal of this struggle whatever little of ourselves we are permitted to give: our lives, our sacrifice, and if some day we have to breathe our last breath on any land, already ours, sprinkled with our blood, let it be known that we have measured the scope of our actions and that we only consider ourselves elements in the great army of the proletariat but that we are proud of having learned from the Cuban Revolution, and from its maximum leader, the great lesson emanating from his attitude in this part of the world: "What do the dangers or the sacrifices of a man or of a nation matter, when the destiny of humanity is at stake."

Our every action is a battle cry against imperialism, and a battle hymn for the people's unity against the great enemy of mankind: the United States of America. Wherever death may surprise us, let it be welcome, provided that this, our battle cry, may have reached some receptive ear and another hand may be extended to wield our weapons and other men be ready to intone the funeral dirge with the staccato singing of the machine guns and new battle cries of war and victory.

SOURCE: Pamphlet, published in English by the Executive Secretariat of the Organization of the Solidarity of the Peoples of Africa, Asia, and Latin America, Havana, April 16, 1967.